The Scriptwriter's Workbook

A Media Writer's Companion

William J. Van Nostran

Focal Press

Boston   Oxford   Johannesburg   Melbourne   New Delhi   Singapore

For Lynne:
Past, Present & Future Tense

Focal Press is an imprint of Butterworth-Heinemann

Ɛ A member of the Reed Elsevier group

Copyright © 1996 by William J. Van Nostran

 Recognizing the importance of preserving what has been written, Butterworth-Heinemann prints its books on acid-free paper whenever possible.

ISBN: 0-240-80273-X

The publisher offers discounts on bulk orders of this book.
For information, please write:

Manager of Special Sales
Butterworth–Heinemann
313 Washington Street
Newton, MA 02158–1626
Tel: 617-928-2500
Fax: 617-928-2620

For information on all Focal Press publications available, contact our World Wide Web home page at: http://www.bh.com/bh/

10 9 8 7 6 5 4 3 2 1

Printed in the United States of America

Table of Contents

List of Figures

How to Use The Scriptwriter's Workbook

This workbook, a companion to *The Scriptwriter's Handbook*, provides students, newcomers to media writing and experienced scriptwriters a step-by-step format for adapting the writing process described in *The Scriptwriter's Handbook* to a specific scriptwriting assignment or project. It can be used for group or individual study.

The workbook contains three types of activities:

- **General Activities**—Exercises to introduce concepts, or enhance awareness of specific media scriptwriting principles.

- **Review Activities**—Cover material presented in specific chapters or sections of *The Scriptwriter's Handbook* text. They are one way of checking your understanding of the material presented in that book. (Review activities do not always appear first in a workbook chapter. Some subjective General Activities are more effective when done as a prelude to reading a chapter.)

- **Scriptwriting Worksheets**—These worksheets provide a step-by-step guide for readers to follow as they develop their own material, working toward a complete, polished shooting script.

From time to time, you'll also encounter:

- **Mini-Lessons**—Short informational blocks of text designed to convey essential information (for those who may not be using *The Scriptwriter's Handbook* text) or, in some cases, additional insights into media scriptwriting.

- **Writing Samples**—Examples to illustrate a writing product at key points in the script development process. (Many more examples are found in *The Scriptwriter's Handbook*.)

If you are working in a classroom setting, many General and Review Activities can be used as a catalyst for class discussion.

Scriptwriting Worksheets, however, relate to each individual's specific writing project or assignment. They will help you plan your writing; identify potential problems and develop feasible solutions so you solve these problems *before* generating a first draft shooting script.

These Scriptwriting Worksheets are not meant to reduce the process to a "paint-by-the-numbers" approach. Instead, by completing each worksheet in sequence, inexperienced media writers are forced to confront key issues at the appropriate stage in the scriptwriting process. Originality and creativity results from how you answer these questions and the insights gained.

EXPERIENCED SCRIPTWRITERS

More experienced writers may find these worksheets useful to consciously explore decisions and writing strategies they usually adopt intuitively. Or, a skilled writer experiencing difficulty or blockage on a project may focus attention on the specific problem and generate potential solutions by using the appropriate project worksheet.

YOUR GOAL

The goal for all media writers is to internalize the generic process of collecting information, analyzing the assignment and audience, conceptualizing and visualizing, drafting and incorporating feedback into revisions. Ultimately, the scriptwriter will rely on intuition, instinct and judgment honed by years of experience.

USING THIS WORKBOOK

Since this is a companion to *The Scriptwriter's Handbook*, it is intended to be used with that text. The *Handbook* explores principles in greater depth and offers many writing examples. This workbook, however, parallels the book's structure:

1. It begins with a general introduction to media and media writing.

2. The bulk of the text, then focuses on the generic scriptwriting process described in detail in *The Scriptwriter's Handbook*:

 • Assimilation

 • Rehearsal

 • Drafting

 • Revision

 • Editing

The Scriptwriters Workbook follows a parallel organization (although it does not provide activities and worksheets for the more specialized types of writing discussed in the final five chapters of *The Scriptwriter's Handbook*). If you use this workbook without *The Scriptwriter's Handbook* for reference, essential content for each segment is found in the "mini-lessons" contained in this workbook.

Separate workbook sections provide suggested answers to each Review and General Activity as well as an Appendix containing a sample project to illustrate use of Scriptwriting Worksheets.

A WORD ON JUDGMENT

Writing is a celebration of diversity and difference. Each writer's solutions to writing problems reflect his or her unique personality. It is not surprising, therefore, that you may not always agree with a workbook answer or with the decisions and results of the sample script in Appendix B.

Psychologist Howard Gardner and writer William Zinsser put it best. Says Gardner:

> "To be able to think in an original way about a topic, a person must have the material so organized in his mind that he can readily juxtapose and combine it in a variety of unexpected ways, proceed in a number of directions with the same information and shuttle with ease from one set of issues to another.
>
> "All these capacities presuppose that the individual can organize information in a number of complex and flexible ways . . . The resulting work is highly individual, idiosyncratic and impervious to formula," writes Gardner.[1]

Characteristically, Zinsser puts it more succinctly: ". . . ultimately the product that any writer has to sell is not his subject, but who he is . . ."[2]

If you have difficulty applying a workbook principle or find that a specific technique does not work for you—don't belabor the point. Move on. All that really matters is what winds up on "the page" and "the screen." How you got there—that's *your* business!

NOTE TO INSTRUCTORS

Just as I encourage scriptwriters to adapt these concepts and strategies to their own writing, I urge classroom teachers to use the text and workbook as a departure point. Adapt, add or delete based on your own experience and expertise, the needs of your students, the instructional goals and your personal teaching style.

Footnotes:
[1] Gardner, Howard, *Art, Mind & Brain*, (New York: Basic Books, Inc., 1982) 261.
[2] Zinsser, William, *On Writing Well*, (Harper & Row, New York, 1980) 5.

CHAPTER 1

Media: A Message

(The Scriptwriter's Handbook, pages 11–28)

GENERAL ACTIVITY 1.1: THINKING ABOUT MEDIA SCRIPTWRITING

WHAT TO DO: Think about media writing as a specific type of writing genre. In many ways, it is no different from other writing genres meant to be read from the printed page.

But there are differences—some subtle, some not so subtle. See how many of these similarities and differences you can generate "off the top of your head" by brainstorming in buzz groups. Enter your ideas in the appropriate column.

Ways in which scriptwriting for media is no different from other genres:	Ways in which scriptwriting for media differs from other writing genres:

What other literary forms or genres is media writing most similar to and why?

_____

_____

REVIEW ACTIVITY

WHAT TO DO: Figures 2.1 through 2.5 in *The Scriptwriter's Handbook* describe the characteristics, strengths and weaknesses of various media. (Workbook Figure 1.1 provides additional data on PC-based multi-media.) To review your understanding of media characteristics, answer the following questions.

1. Put a "P" by those media which create and display visual images photographically, an "E" by those that create and display visuals electronically, and "NA" by those which do not apply:
   _____ Print
   _____ Audio Cassette
   _____ Videotape
   _____ Multi-Image Slide Presentations
   _____ Film
   _____ PC-Based Multi-Media

2. Put an "M" by all those media which are full-motion media:
   _____ Print
   _____ Audio Cassette
   _____ Videotape
   _____ Multi-Image Slide Presentations
   _____ Film
   _____ PC-Based Multi-Media

3. The illusion of motion results from a phenomenon known as: _____

4. Identify the full motion medium associated with the following frames per second. Place "NA" by any that do not apply.
   24 frames per second _____
   26 frames per second _____
   30 frames per second _____
   32 frames per second _____

5. Place a "1" by those media having the best image resolution:
   _____ Video
   _____ Film
   _____ 35mm slides
   _____ PC-based multi-media

6. Place a check-mark by those media which provide immediate recording and playback capability:
   _____ Video
   _____ Film
   _____ Multi-Media Slide Presentation
   _____ Audio Cassette
   _____ PC-Based Multi-Media
   _____ Print

7. Place a check-mark by those media which generally require some type of computer programming or special authoring to create and playback the finished product:

____ Multi-Image Slide Presentation

____ Film

____ PC-Based Multi-Media

____ Audio Cassette

____ Video Teleconference

____ Videowall Presentation

8. Place a check-mark by those media which are ideally suited for viewing by a large audience of 100 people or more:

____ Film

____ Print

____ Multi-Image Slide Presentation

____ Audio Cassette

____ PC-Based Multi-Media

____ Video

9. Place a check-mark by those media which are ideally suited for a one-on-one sales presentation in the customer's office:

____ Film

____ Print

____ Multi-Image Slide Presentation

____ Audio Cassette

____ PC-Based Multi-Media

____ Video

10. What is a "hybrid" medium? Give at least one example.

_____

_____

_____

11. Why is it necessary for a writer to know the characteristics, strengths and weaknesses of various media?

_____

_____

_____

Figure 1
PC-Based Multi-Media

CHARACTERISTICS

- Combines personal computer technology with text, graphics, visuals, audio and, in some formats, full-motion video.

- Random access capabilities allow user to interact directly with on-screen information, accessing data or information on a "need-to-know" basis.

- Non-linear branching capabilities provide program developers opportunity to present content as "scenarios" with multiple outcomes based on path selected by user. You "tell yourself" a story by interacting with the content.

STRENGTHS

- High degree of user participation and involvement makes multi-media ideal for meeting training objectives with technical subject matter such as medical, financial and other complex, abstract subjects.

- Efficient way to communicate and train since each user makes individual choices regarding what information to access and how deeply to explore each topic.

- Permits pre- and post-diagnostic testing with capability to send user to appropriate remedial learning components.

- Allows program design team to make optimal match between content and media (i.e., use of motion, animation, text, graphics, sound, etc.)

- Similarity to video game technology provides opportunity for incorporating entertainment value into program design.

- Easily installed and adapted to kiosk settings for public access or trade show/convention floor use.

WEAKNESSES

- Additional media and software design, authoring, programming and testing results in longer production lead times than for traditional linear media.

- Users require computer hardware with compatible multi-media capabilities. (CD-ROM disk drive, for example.)

- Not suited to large audience display or interaction.

- Not easily updated.

SPECIAL CONSIDERATIONS FOR WRITER:

- Writers must organize content in non-linear, random access modes to capitalize on interactive branching potential.

- Need to work with new design tools (flowcharts, etc.) and interact with additional personnel such as software programmers.

- Need to know capabilities of appropriate hardware and software authoring platforms.

- Requires flexibility, versatility and imagination to capitalize on full range of available media in various combinations and the potential for differing interactions.

SCRIPTWRITING WORKSHEET 1:
SELECTING THE MEDIUM FOR THE MESSAGE

BACKGROUND: As scriptwriter, sometimes you'll take part in media selection—identifying which medium is best suited to the needs of a given project.

Other times, the medium will be chosen by the client, producer or others before your involvement as writer.

In either case, the writer must consider how various aspects of the assignment (subject matter, objectives, audience, program shelf-life, etc.) are affected by the medium. Answering the following questions will help stimulate such thinking about your own project.

WHAT TO DO: Answer the following questions as they relate to your specific project.

1. If you have no say in what medium you'll be writing for, enter that medium below:

   _____

   [If media selection is part of your assignment, skip ahead to question 4:]

2. Referring to the appropriate media chart on pages 16 through 28 in *The Scriptwriter's Handbook*, what specific strengths of this medium are likely to be most advantageous given what you know so far about the assignment?

   _____

   _____

   _____

   _____

3. Referring to this same media chart, what specific weaknesses of this medium are likely to work against you given what you know so far about the assignment?

   _____

   _____

   _____

   _____

   _____

(Answer the next questions *only* if you are involved in media selection:)

4. If you have a say in what medium is selected for this project/assignment, return to this page to consider these questions *after* completing all the activities up to and including Chapter 4: Organizing Information.

    a. Given the nature of your content, what media seem best suited to deliver this message?

        _____

        _____

        _____

    b. Explain why

        _____

        _____

        _____

    c. Given your *audience*, *viewing environment* and *objectives*, what media seem best suited to deliver this message?

        _____

        _____

    d. Explain why

        _____

        _____

        _____

5. Consider these additional factors:

    a. How long a shelf-life is your project expected to have?

        _____

    b. During this program's lifetime, is the information likely to change frequently?

        _____ Yes   _____ No

    c. How will budget and/or production facilities/resources affect media selection?

_____

_____

_____

    d. Does the due date affect media selection? If so, how?

_____

_____

6. Considering *all* factors, what is your medium of choice for this assignment?

_____

Why? _____

_____

7. If, for some reason, you are unable to write for your medium of choice, what medium would be the best alternative?

_____

Why? _____

_____

_____

8. After considering all these factors and discussing them with the client and producer as appropriate, what medium has been selected for your project?

_____

NEXT...

Answer questions 1 through 3 and return to the script development process. Or, if you've answered those questions already, move ahead to begin the script development process.

2

The Scriptwriting Process

(The Scriptwriter's Handbook, pages 29–33)

GENERAL ACTIVITY 2.1: THE WRITING PROCESS

PURPOSE: This activity introduces the scriptwriting process that will be followed throughout *The Scriptwriter's Workbook.*

WHAT TO DO: Think about steps you take when doing *any* writing. You do not need to refer to a media script. You can refer to the process you use for print writing, news stories, articles, promotional copy, a training program, term papers—even letters (preferably a formal letter with a specific purpose rather than an impromptu letter to a friend or relative).

What do you do first, second, third, etc.? Jot down the steps you take in the space below. You could also do this in collaboration with a classroom partner.

Step 1: _____

Step 2: _____

Step 3: _____

Step 4: _____

Step 5: _____

Step 6: _____

Step 7: _____

Step 8: _____

Additional Steps:

REVIEW ACTIVITY 2: THE WRITING PROCESS

PURPOSE: Steps in the generic writing process are no different than the steps involved in the creation of a media script. However, the writing products, the purposes they serve, and the visualization skills and format used to communicate your ideas may be new to you. The following activity reviews the writing process explained on pages 29-33 of *The Scriptwriter's Handbook*. Complete the activity as a way of reviewing your understanding of this process.

WHAT TO DO: The following is a list of writing *products* which conclude each major stage of the script-writing process. Fill in the blanks by describing the stage of the media writing process they are associated with. Then answer the questions that follow:

Content Outline_____

Media Treatment_____

Audience Profile _____

Revised Shooting Script _____

Objectives _____

First Draft Shooting Script _____

Completed Shooting Script_____

DEFINITIONS: **Assimilation**—Includes research but also involves the synthesis necessary to make a subject one's own.

Rehearsal—At this stage, the writer focuses on creative possibilities; how best to use media to present content in an interesting, engaging manner. The writer's goal is to develop a creative treatment.

Drafting—The writer's primary goal is to generate a rough, first draft production script.

Revision—Literally, to "see again." The writer incorporates feedback from client, content experts, producer, director and others.

Editing—Incorporating final changes and polishing the script prior to production.

1. At what stage of the scriptwriting process would it be appropriate to hear this comment from the client:

   "I don't like this approach at all. It's too serious a subject to be treated with humor."

   Stage in process: _____

   Why? Justify your answer.

   _____

   _____

   At what stage would it be inappropriate to hear such a comment? _____

   Why? Justify your answer.

   _____

   _____

2. An in-house producer tells you:

   "I've been concerned about this approach all along. But now that I see it fully scripted, I have to say—I don't think it's appropriate for our organization."

   Stage in the process: _____

   Is this an appropriate stage in the process to hear this response? _____

   Why? Justify your answer.

   _____

   _____

GENERAL ACTIVITY 2.2: FUNCTIONS OF THE MEDIA SCRIPT

WHAT TO DO: What is the purpose of a media script? In reality, it serves several functions. In the space provided, "brainstorm" as many functions of a media script as you can think of. If in a class, work in small groups.

Functions of a media script include:

_____

_____

_____

_____

_____

_____

_____

_____

_____

_____

DEFINITION: **Script**—A script is the written description of a chronological sequence of events, identifying sounds, pictures and ideas, using media production terminology.

GENERAL ACTIVITY 2.3: IDENTIFYING SCRIPT READERS

PURPOSE: Ultimately, all scripts have built-in obsolescence. The finished production renders the script obsolete.

There are, however, several important people who do read our scripts prior to production. This activity gets you thinking about who those people are and the perspective they bring to evaluating your script.

WHAT TO DO: In the first column, identify by title those people who will be reading your script.

In the second column, write down the perspective of each reader. What will they be focusing on most when they read: content, style, production feasibility, visualization, etc.?

In the final column, consider how skilled each reader is in interpreting the script as a media experience. Can they visualize? Will they get a sense of timing and pace? Will they be able to "see and hear" the program from the printed page? If the reader is skilled at reading scripts, circle "skilled." If not, circle "unskilled."

Identify SCRIPT READERS by TITLE: This READER will focus on:

_____   _____ skilled/unskilled

_____   _____ skilled/unskilled

_____   _____ skilled/unskilled

_____   _____ skilled/unskilled

_____   _____ skilled/unskilled

_____   _____ skilled/unskilled

Remember, these readers are usually not members of the viewing audience. Ultimately, we write to communicate with viewers or listeners.

One of the challenges and tensions in media writing is to reconcile comments and feedback of script readers with the needs of our viewing audience.

During the first phase of the scriptwriting process, Assimilation, we will gain insight into the needs of both client and our audience. . .

Collecting Information for the Script

(The Scriptwriter's Handbook, pages 35–52)

GENERAL ACTIVITY 3.1: WHAT MAKES THE DIFFERENCE?

Think of a time you were personally "invested" in a piece of writing. It may be a letter, a poem, a report, a corporate memo. Jot down reasons *why* you connected with this piece of writing	Think of a time you did not "connect" with a piece of writing. As a result, the writing was difficult and tedious. Jot down reasons why you found this writing a chore.

Writing Experience:

_____

Reasons:

_____

_____

_____

_____

_____

_____

Writing Experience:

_____

Reasons:

_____

_____

_____

_____

_____

_____

Now, answer this question: What made the difference?

_____

_____

_____

REVIEW ACTIVITY: THE ASSIMILATION STEP

WHAT TO DO: Answer the following questions. . .

1. What are the three main goals of research?

_____

_____

_____

2. What is the "core question?"

_____

_____

_____

3. How does the "core question" relate to the three main goals of research?

_____   _____

_____   _____

_____   _____

4. There are many ways to conduct research. Brainstorm various methods the inquiring scriptwriter can use to gather useful information about the topic or assignment.

_____   _____

_____   _____

_____   _____

_____   _____

5. What is the difference between "research" and "assimilation?"

_____

_____

_____

6. What are some signs that you have collected sufficient information to proceed to the next step of the scriptwriting process?

_____

_____

_____

7. Why is the assimilation process important to the writer?

_____

_____

_____

WRITING PRODUCT 1: THE RESEARCH AGENDA

DEFINITION: **Research Agenda**—A list of the specific interviews, readings, observations, etc. you must accomplish in order to collect the information necessary.

PURPOSE: The Research Agenda is a tool the scriptwriter uses to:

- organize the research task

- evaluate progress

- a Research Agenda can also be useful as a tool for slowing down the over-anxious client who presses you for an immediate creative concept

The next page provides a sample of a Research Agenda, followed by a Scriptwriting Worksheet for use in helping to organize the research task for your own project.

The sample Research Agenda is for a technical training video script to teach new operators how to work with a large machine tool press.

21

Figure 2
SAMPLE: RESEARCH AGENDA

Program Title: Introduction to 80-Ton Machine Tool Press

Contact	*Activity*

Process Engineer
(Content Expert)
	Interview & Observation
	Will provide overview of products machined on the 80-Ton V&O press and explain three specific operations:
	   • Notch
	   • Hole-Punching
	   • Trim
	Will explain importance of the process to the finished product and how defects detract from product quality and add to production costs and operating time.
	
	Reading
	Will provide quality control benchmark standards for all machine operators.
	Will provide statistics correlating quality problems to production costs.

Manufacturing Engineer
(Program User)
	Interview & Observation
	Will point out major parts on the 80-Ton V&O press.
	Will demonstrate proper procedure for:
	   • Loading & unloading product
	   • How to start & stop press
	   • How to cycle press
	Overview safety procedures and production handling requirements.
	Describe current On-the-Job-Training (OJT) procedures.
	
	Reading
	Will provide copy of current operating manual.

Recently Trained New Operator (Target Audience)	*Interview* Probe to get understanding of initial impression of the job. Describe any problems/concerns they had running the press as new hire. Probe for understanding of how thoroughly they understand how finished parts relate to overall process and need for quality. What would they suggest video training package include?
Experienced Operator (One responsible for OJT)	*Interview/Demonstration* Describe how a new operator is taught to run the press. Find out what is most difficult for new operators. *Observation* Watch a new operator being taught to run the press.

SCRIPTWRITING WORKSHEET 2:
YOUR RESEARCH AGENDA

PROJECT: _____

Develop a List of Interview Contacts   *What do you expect to learn from the Interview?*

1. _____   _____

2. _____   _____

3. _____   _____

4. _____   _____

5. _____   _____

6. _____   _____

7. _____   _____

8. _____   _____

Time Frame for Completion: _____

Develop A List of Readings & Resource Materials

_____

_____

_____

_____

_____

_____

_____

_____

Time Frame for Completion: _____

Develop a List of Activities You'll Need to Do or See

1. _____

2. _____

3. _____

4. _____

5. _____

6. _____

7. _____

Time Frame for Completion: _____

Will Questionnaires or Surveys Be Useful in Learning More About the Content, Organization or Audience?

_____ Yes   _____ No

If "yes", describe the purpose of the Questionnaire or Survey?

_____

_____

_____

Will you have the time and resources to conduct this research activity?

_____ Yes   _____ No

Time Frame for Completion: _____

Other Research Activities

_____

_____

_____

Time Frame for Completion: _____

C H A P T E R **4**

Organizing Information

(The Scriptwriter's Handbook, pages 53–70)

INTRODUCTION

"All writing begins in confusion." Now is when you slowly begin making sense of the chaos. In the next phase of the Assimilation process, you analyze and organize the raw material gathered during research and begin shaping it for yourself, your client, the subject matter expert and the producer.

The remaining writing products resulting from the Assimilation step are ways of "feeding back" your understanding of the assignment and initial research results to the client. Not yet scripts by any means, these documents verify your understanding of the program's intended audience, objectives and content.

This ensures that the creative strategy you develop in the Rehearsal Step is based on a firm, solid foundation—an understanding of "what the client wants to say, to whom, and for what purpose."

REVIEW ACTIVITY: ORGANIZING INFORMATION

PURPOSE: The following activity reviews the concepts explained in Chapter 4 of *The Scriptwriter's Handbook*. Complete the activity as a way of reviewing your understanding of how to translate research results into an action plan.

WHAT TO DO: Answer the following questions. . .

1. Your Action Plan begins with three important writing products:

    • Audience Profile

    • Objectives

    • Content Outline

What is the overall purpose of these three documents?

_____

_____

_____

2. How does the audience's pre-disposition toward the subject matter of the communication influence the scriptwriter's task?

_____

_____

_____

_____

3. How does the viewing situation influence the scriptwriter's task?

_____

_____

_____

_____

4. What are four types of media program objectives and how do they differ?

Type of Objective	Characteristics
_____	_____
	_____
_____	_____
	_____
_____	_____
	_____
_____	_____

5. How does a content outline for a media script *differ* from content outlines for more traditional types of print writing assignments?

_____

_____

_____

WRITING PRODUCT 2: AUDIENCE PROFILE AND VIEWING ENVIRONMENT

DEFINITION: The Audience Profile is a description of the intended audience and relevant information regarding the communication environment and viewing situation. Here is an example:

Figure 3
SAMPLE AUDIENCE PROFILE

"The audience is the pharmaceutical sales force. During the past 18 months, the home office has placed a priority on physician sales calls. In this video program, we will be asking the sales force to build inventories at the retail pharmacy level. Unless the message is properly positioned, the sales force could perceive this as a case of conflicting priorities and poor coordination."

BACKGROUND: Your perception of the audience is also closely related to the viewing environment. How is this program meant to be seen? By an individual viewer? By a class? By a huge audience on a large screen?

Will the program be seen in the home? At work? In a doctor's office? At a conference or meeting? A trade show exhibit floor?

Will you have a captive audience, or will you have to vie for their attention? Will they be looking forward to the viewing experience? Is the program communicating good news, bad news or a mixture?

Will the audience be active participants or passive viewers? Will there be other materials they will interact with such as workbooks, computer software, simulators, etc.?

Through the Audience Profile, you let the client know you understand and appreciate the dynamics of the communication environment. And, if your client perceives the audience and communication environment differently, now is the time to find out; not after you've invested time and energy writing a complete script.

SCRIPTWRITING WORKSHEET 3: YOUR AUDIENCE PROFILE

WHAT TO DO: Write your initial understanding of the audience and the logistics of the "communication environment" in the space provided:

_____

_____

_____

_____

_____

Assess the communication environment. Knowing what you do about the audience, the message and the dynamics of the viewing environment, is your viewing audience likely to be:

_____ Positive

_____ Neutral

_____ Negative

What factors lead you to this conclusion?

_____

_____

_____

_____

After completing your research: Double-check your initial understanding of the audience and communication environment. Has it changed? If so, revise as necessary:

A Warning about Multiple Audiences:

Whenever a client asks you to write one script to reach more than *one* audience—make it quite clear what can and cannot be communicated with a single media presentation.

Your script cannot be all things to all audiences. What you say to a sales force is probably not what you'd say to prospective customers about the same product. The way you speak to doctors is quite different from the way you address patients—even discussing the same medical condition.

Generally, multiple audiences complicate the writing and/or production process. Often, you'll need two versions of the same script and finished program. Although producing two versions of similar content usually involves some economies of scale, it is almost always more expensive than producing one program targeted to a single, homogeneous audience.

[For more on writing to multiple audiences, see *The Scriptwriter's Handbook*, Chapter 4, pages 57 to 59.]

WRITING SAMPLE 3: PROGRAM OBJECTIVES

BACKGROUND: Objectives establish the client's expectations for the completed program. Be specific and realistic in establishing objectives—they become the "benchmark" for assessing a program's effectiveness.

Most programs involve these types of objectives:

Informational Objective: The audience is not required to act on information presented in the program.

Behavioral Objective (Also known as **Instructional Objectives**): Seeks to achieve specific, demonstrable and/or observable changes in the audience that can be measured through pre and post-testing.

Motivational Objective: The end behavior of motivational objectives is less specific than for instructional objectives—yet a definite response to subject matter is sought.

Figure 4
SAMPLE: PROGRAM OBJECTIVES

Informational Objective:
Show children who have just been diagnosed with epilepsy how other children have learned to live with their seizure disorders.

Motivational Objective:
Encourage improved communication between Sales Representatives in the field and Customer Service Representatives to achieve a higher level of prompt customer service and satisfaction.

Instructional Objectives:

NOTE: When writing behavioral objectives, state the changes which the program intends to effect on the target audience. For example:

Unit Objective
Upon completion of this unit, the trainee will be able to type, store, recall and modify correspondence, reports, forms and other materials using the Memory Save/Recall features of the "Letter Perfect" word processing software program.

Sub Objectives
To achieve the overall objective, content and exercises will be structured so participants will be able to:

- Enter data into "Memory Store".

- Recall data from "Memory Store".

- Make changes to data and save the revised document in "Memory Store."

GENERAL ACTIVITY 4.1: IDENTIFYING PROGRAM OBJECTIVES

WHAT TO DO: Read through the list of program subjects. Although not phrased as specific objectives, most can be fairly typically classified as a media project with either an informational, motivational or behavioral objective. Write the type of objective you think each program best exemplifies in the space provided. Is the program primarily informational, instructional or motivational in nature?

1. A videotape on what constitutes sexual harassment: _____

    _____

2. A corporate television news program: _____

    _____

3. A short multi-image module on leadership to kick-off a management conference:

    _____

4. A videotape introducing company benefits to new employees:_____

    _____

5. An audio cassette providing general background on epilepsy for individuals who have just been diagnosed as having epilepsy:

    _____

6. A multi-media computer program on how to use advanced, high-end accounting software:

    _____

In doing this activity, you may have felt some of the topics would probably involve more than one type of objective. Very often—this is the case. Training programs, for instance, impart information and the participants must be motivated to stay actively involved and do their best.

Before moving on, consider one other type of objective: entertainment. Writers of theatrical motion pictures or sit-coms are primarily seeking to entertain an audience. But what role, if any, does entertainment value play in writing corporate or organizational media scripts?

WHAT TO DO: Answer the following questions:

7. Is there a role for entertainment in corporate or instructional media program design?

                    ____ Yes   ____ No

8. Justify your response in the space provided:

_____

_____

_____

_____

_____

_____

SCRIPTWRITING WORKSHEET 4: YOUR PROGRAM OBJECTIVES

WHAT TO DO: Describe the overall, primary objective of your program in your own words:

_____

_____

_____

_____

_____

How would you categorize the primary objective? Check the appropriate type:

____ Informational

____ Motivational

____ Instructional

In what ways, if any, will your program have to be motivational as well as informational or instructional?

_____

_____

_____

_____

_____

GENERAL ACTIVITY 4.2: FOCUSING ON CRITICAL CONTENT

BACKGROUND: Typically, you accumulate much more material than can be included in your script. So what criteria do you use to select what to include and what to exclude?

"Critical content focusing" is one approach to making this decision. As you begin organizing material, most will fall into one of four categories:

- Critical Content

- Supporting Points

- "Nice to Know" Information

- Unnecessary Content

Begin by trying to identify and focus on the critical content that absolutely must be included.

WHAT TO DO: List criteria you can use to evaluate the information you've collected during research to determine the critical content points.

_____

_____

_____

_____

_____

SCRIPTWRITING WORKSHEET 5: YOUR CRITICAL CONTENT

PURPOSE: Another way to think of critical content: it is the two, three or four key points you want your audience to *remember*. That means these must become the most memorable moments in your script. (Or, if you're designing a major training program with many modules, the critical content consists of the most important learning objectives in each module.)

It's vital to know the critical content because you build your "big scenes" around these content points. Everything else supports or enhances—but should never overshadow.

WHAT TO DO: To help identify the critical content of your program, answer the following questions. If you have difficulty completing this worksheet, you may not have sufficiently assimilated the content yet. Try to determine what areas you should research further.

1. List factors that tend to make your target audience *receptive* to the message.

   _____

   _____

   _____

2. What factors, if any, might make the target audience respond *negatively* to the content or message?

   _____

   _____

   _____

3. If you were a member of the viewing audience, what would *you* like to get out of this program?

   _____

   _____

   _____

4. How can you appeal to the self-interest of your audience to generate interest in the program?

   _____

   _____

   _____

5. Given your assessment of the objectives, the audience and the communication environment, what three to five content points are *most* critical? (Once you identify these topics, you must find ways to communicate these points effectively. Ideally, they become the *big* moments in the finished program.)

   _____

   _____

   _____

   _____

   _____

   _____

   _____

WRITING PRODUCT 4: THE CONTENT OUTLINE

BACKGROUND: Now that you've identified the "Critical Content", use these points as the main topic sentences to create a content outline. Fill in the outline with supporting points under the appropriate headings. The content outline is another important checkpoint document for writer, client and subject matter expert.

Notice that the following Sample Outline makes no reference to how the material will be treated *creatively* by the scriptwriter for the chosen medium. Content Outlines focus solely on what the program is going to be *about*. Since content should always drive form—creative decisions must come after you have determined what the program is about.

Figure 5
SAMPLE: CONTENT OUTLINE

I. Product/Market Overview

    A. Product Integrity—Corporeal Diagnostics offers best blood gas analyzer quality control product on the market. Claim backed by experience and third party endorsements.

    B. Ease of Use—Product stores conveniently. Test procedures simple to follow. Designed for use on all blood gas instruments.

    C. Customer Service—Corporeal Diagnostics offers widest range of useful, comprehensive support services.

II. In light of this, how can competition be penetrating the market with inferior products?

    A. Product features are not perceived as benefits by the customer.

        1. Example: A less sensitive product may give the lab a false sense of confidence in their instruments.

        2. Example: Statistical data may be meaningless to a customer who cannot interpret raw data.

        3. Example: Customer may not appreciate need for accurate values at different levels.

    B. These and other typical objections can be overcome through customer education. Competitive feature/benefit story must be directly related to needs and concerns of specific target accounts. This training module teaches a strategy for doing just that. . .

C H A P T E R **5**

Idea Development

(The Scriptwriter's Handbook, pages 73–118)

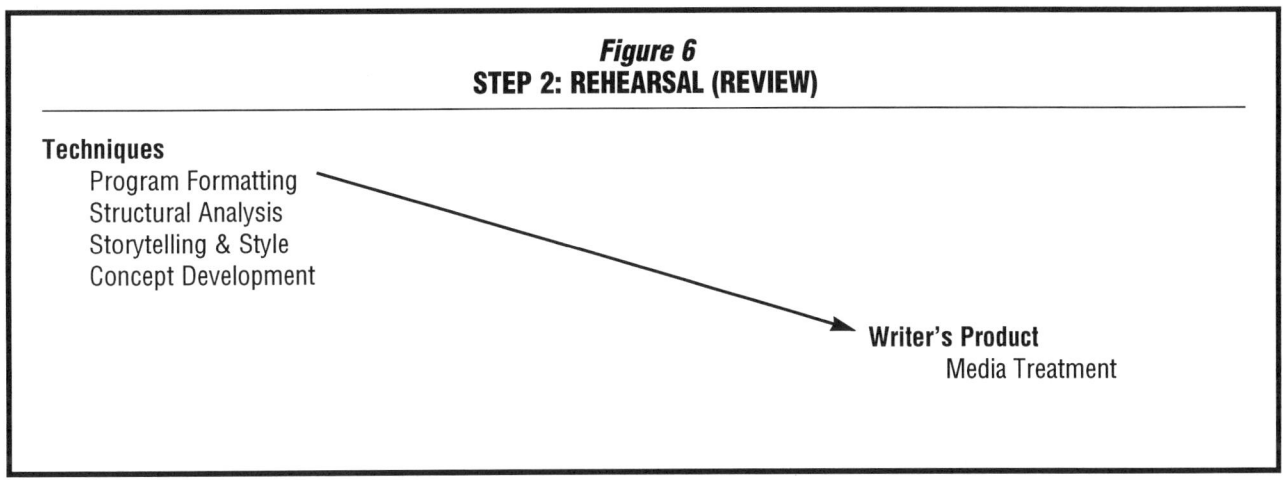

Figure 6
STEP 2: REHEARSAL (REVIEW)

Techniques
Program Formatting
Structural Analysis
Storytelling & Style
Concept Development

Writer's Product
Media Treatment

MINI-LESSON: THE REHEARSAL PHASE

Actress Julie Harris once told a master class: "in the hustle and bustle of rehearsal, it's important to leave time for the *daydreaming* part." This is good advice for writers as well—especially at this stage in the process. Now that we have a thorough understanding of what the media program will be *about* it's time to focus on communicating that content creatively using the strengths of the chosen medium.

With the press of deadlines and meetings that usually go with writing a script, it's vital to allocate some time to the *daydreaming* part. The Rehearsal phase of the writing process is the writer's opportunity for exploring possibilities, for asking the question: "What if?"

Rehearsal is your time to consider the array of creative choices open to you. Because there are so many choices to consider, it may seem overwhelming at first. Through the next few activities and scriptwriting worksheets, we'll simplify the task by focusing on various aspects of a creative concept:

• program formats

• structure

• style

• storytelling principles

• concept development

These are decisions a scriptwriter must make anew each and every time out. Completing the scriptwriting worksheets will force you to make these decisions consciously and early in the writing process.

Experienced scriptwriters often arrive at these decisions intuitively. But even experienced writers are sometimes blocked creatively. When that occurs, the following scriptwriting worksheets may help provide new insight, generating fresh creative territory to explore.

First, we'll examine the elements that constitute a creative concept individually. Then, we'll see how your creative concept pulls them all together, resulting in a unified, aesthetically pleasing whole.

GENERAL ACTIVITY 5.1: THE SCRIPTWRITER'S CHOICES

WHAT TO DO: Consider some of the many choices media scriptwriters must make—not choices regarding the content of the program, but choices relating to the creative treatment of the material as a viewing, listening or interactive experience.

Brainstorm a list of the kinds of choices media writers must make before beginning to draft a script.

_____

_____

_____

_____

REVIEW ACTIVITY: IDEA DEVELOPMENT

WHAT TO DO: Answer the following questions. Feel free to refer back to the Idea Development chapter when necessary.

1. Professional writer and teacher of writing Donald Murray made an important discovery when he allowed a colleague to study his writing methodology. Fill in the blanks below. If you don't recall the exact percentages, take a guess—then return to the Idea Development chapter to see how close you were to the actual findings.

Amount of writing time Murray spent collecting information and planning:

_____

Amount of time Murray actually spent writing:

_____

What is the significance of this finding to all writers?

_____

_____

2. William Goldman is quoted discussing the importance of structure in writing screenplays. Structure is equally important to the media writer. What three decisions does the scriptwriter make when determining the proper structure for a script?

A. What material to _____.

B. What material to _____.

C. The _____ of that material from _____ to _____.

3. List several different points of view a writer can take in expressing the identical content:

_____

_____

_____

_____

4. Peter Elbow describes a paradox that exists in all creative work: "Writing calls on two skills that are so different they usually conflict with each other: creating and criticizing."

Describe the role of the creative child or artist during the rehearsal phase:

_____

_____

Describe the role of the adult judge or critic during the rehearsal phase:

_____

_____

How can the writer keep from having the adult critic stifle the imagination of the creative child?

_____

_____

5. Describe the difference between a media treatment and a media *script*:

_____

_____

_____

GENERAL ACTIVITY 5.2: MEDIA PROGRAM FORMATS

WHAT TO DO: A **format** is a generic method of presenting information through audiovisual media. Formats exist independently of content, style and structure. Content may be presented in any format the writer chooses—although some formats may be more suited to specific content than others.

Before deciding what format or mix of formats is best for your subject, consider the pros and cons of these six generic program formats. Enter your thoughts in the space provided for each generic format.

Format 1: Talking Head

Definition: Speakers who address the camera and deliver content without any visualization.

Pros	Cons

Format 2: Talking Head with Props

Definition: An on-camera speaker who addresses the camera while working with props or other visuals to help communicate the message.

Pros	Cons

Format 3: Visuals & Voice

Definition: An off-camera voice with simultaneous display of related visual content or images. (This is the typical sound-slide show format. Can also be a multi-image or computer-generated presentation.) The combined effect of pictures and sound should work synergistically.

Pros	Cons

Format 4A: Interview (*On-camera*)

Definition: The on-camera interview features *both* the interviewer and the interviewee.

Pros	Cons

Format 4B: Interview (*Off-camera*)

Definition: The off-camera interview features only the subject and his/her answers. Interviewer questions are edited out.

Pros	Cons

Format 5: Dramatization

Definition: Content is scripted as dialogue for actors to deliver by assuming the identity of a *character*. Ideally, should involve conflict between characters.

Pros	Cons
_____	_____
_____	_____
_____	_____
_____	_____
_____	_____
_____	_____

Format 6: "Apples & Oranges"

Definition: A free-flowing mixture of two or more of the above formats to meet the communication or training needs of the subject matter and add contrast.

Pros	Cons
_____	_____
_____	_____
_____	_____
_____	_____
_____	_____
_____	_____

SCRIPTWRITING WORKSHEET 6: MATCHING FORMATS TO YOUR CONTENT

WHAT TO DO: Refer to your content outline. Select the key points of the presentation and enter each below. Then, for each key point, determine the Program Format you think will be most *effective* and enter in the space provided.

In addition, identify a Program Format that could be used as an *alternate* method of presenting the same key point.

Key Point 1: _____

Most Effective Format: _____

Alternate Format: _____

Key Point 2: _____

       Most Effective Format: _____

       Alternate Format: _____

Key Point 3: _____

       Most Effective Format: _____

       Alternate Format: _____

Key Point 4: _____

       Most Effective Format: _____

       Alternate Format: _____

Key Point 5: _____

       Most Effective Format: _____

       Alternate Format: _____

PART 2

WHAT TO DO: Now, answer the following questions by reviewing the selections you made for each key point.

1. Looking at the "Most Effective" formats, is there any danger your script will lack variety in format?

           _____ Yes   _____ No

If you marked "Yes". . .

Review the list of "Alternative Formats." Can you identify a logical solution?

           _____ Yes

Describe your solution:

_____

_____

_____

_____ No

Explain why the "Alternative Formats" fail to solve the problem you anticipate:

_____

_____

_____

_____

_____

If you marked "No" for question 1, review the list of "Most Effective" Formats. Is there any danger of your script resulting in a "hodge-podge" of formats, with no single format dominating?

_____ Yes

In this case, review the list of "Alternative Formats" to see if there is a solution to this problem.

Describe your solution:

_____

_____

_____

_____

_____

_____ No

In this case, explain why the formats you are combining will be compatible with one another:

_____

_____

_____

_____

_____

GENERAL ACTIVITY 5.3:
ADVERTISED OR UNADVERTISED PROGRAM STRUCTURE

BACKGROUND: Structure is a planned framework for revealing the chronological sequence of events on screen.

By nature, structuring content is a selective process. You already determined what content to include and what to exclude through critical content focusing. Now you make decisions on the placement of that material from beginning to end.

Sometimes, you'll want to **advertise** the structure to your audience—using verbal and visual signposts to guide them through content.

WHAT TO DO: Brainstorm tools the scriptwriter can use to advertise the program structure to the audience. Think of it as ways of letting the audience know what is coming next and reminding them of where they are throughout the time span of the viewing or listening experience.

_____

_____

_____

_____

_____

_____

For other scripts, you'll want to use the element of surprise by concealing the structure. There is still an underlying structure and order—but when **unadvertised,** it is not readily apparent to the audience what will happen next.

Brainstorm techniques you can use to conceal the structure:

_____

_____

_____

_____

_____

_____

_____

WHAT TO DO: Think about the advantages and disadvantages of advertising the structure to your audience and list below. Then, do the same for the unadvertised structure:

Programs using an *advertised* structure...

Advantages	Disadvantages

Programs using an *unadvertised* structure...

Advantages	Disadvantages

GENERAL ACTIVITY 5.4: MAJOR SEGMENTS OF PROGRAM STRUCTURE

BACKGROUND: Media scripts for film and video are produced one scene at a time—shot by shot. Since all scenes in one location, studio environment or using the same on-camera talent are generally shot together to maximize production efficiency, programs are not necessarily produced in chronological sequence.

    The media writer, however, always thinks in terms of the flow of the final, edited program. The final viewing or listening experience will have an opening, a body that may consist of several scenes to develop content, and a closing.

WHAT TO DO: Brainstorm the functions of each of these major program elements. What should you try to accomplish in your opening, body and closing scenes?

Opening Scenes:

_____

_____

_____

_____

Scenes Comprising the Body:

_____

_____

_____

_____

Closing Scenes:

_____

_____

_____

_____

SCRIPTWRITING WORKSHEET 7:
DETERMINING YOUR PROGRAM'S STRUCTURE

WHAT TO DO: Answer the following questions with your own scriptwriting project in mind.

1. Referring to your program objectives, audience analysis and critical content, which structural type best suits the needs of your program?

    _____ Advertised structure

    _____ Unadvertised structure

    _____ A combination of the two

2A. (Answer if you intend to make the program structure apparent to the audience.) Why will **advertising** the structure work to your advantage in achieving the program's objectives?

    _____

    _____

    _____

    _____

    What visual or narrative cues and techniques could you employ to advertise the structure and provide reference points as the program unfolds?

    _____

    _____

    _____

    _____

2B. (Answer only if you choose to **conceal** the program structure from the audience.) Why will an **unadvertised** structure work to your advantage in achieving the program's objectives?

    _____

    _____

    _____

    _____

What visual/narrative technique will you use to keep the audience "off-balance," unable to predict what will happen next?

_____

_____

_____

_____

To keep the program from appearing random and haphazard, your script must still have an underlying structure or "spine" which the writer and director can follow. Describe the underlying structure of your program:

_____

_____

_____

_____

3. Next, consider these questions about the chronological sequence of events that will unfold on screen.
   A. Think about the critical content that will become major scenes in your script. Use key words to describe these "big" scenes and list them below.

_____

_____

_____

_____

   B. Can you think of a way to open the program that meets the requirements of a good opening scene or sequence of scenes? If so, describe below:

_____

_____

_____

_____

If you're unsure about how to open the program—don't get stuck on the question. You can make this decision later.

C. What is your script building toward? What is the climax? The high point? Describe a closing scene or sequence that meets the requirements of a strong closing:

_____

_____

_____

_____

GENERAL ACTIVITY 5.5
SEARCHING FOR AN APPROPRIATE WAY TO TELL YOUR STORY

BACKGROUND: Storytelling is a powerful way to humanize your message—to take dry facts and information and make them meaningful to your target audience.

Storytelling has been getting lots of play in management circles. In a book titled *Management by Storying Around,* Armstrong International's president writes: "Storytelling changes the way you manage... That's because telling stories is friendly and enjoyable... It's a great way of explaining to people what needs to be done without saying: 'Do this.'"

In *Lincoln on Leadership,* Donald Phillips devotes a chapter to Abe Lincoln's storytelling. "They say I tell a great many stories," said Lincoln. "I reckon I do; but I have learned from long experience that plain people... are more easily influenced through the medium of a broad and humorous illustration than in any other way..."

The best media writers become spinners of interesting and vivid yarns—finding ways to connect with their audience.

WHAT TO DO: There are different kinds of stories as well as different ways to tell a story. Develop a list of each in the appropriate column.

Kinds of Stories:	Ways to tell a story:

SCRIPTWRITING WORKSHEET 8: DO YOU HAVE A STORY TO TELL?

WHAT TO DO: Referring to your own content, audience and objectives, brainstorm ways to humanize the message through storytelling techniques.

1. What kind of a story do I have to tell?

    _____

    _____

    _____

    _____

2. Do you feel a need to humanize this message?

    _____ Yes   _____ No

    If "yes," what are some ways to surprise your audience through vivid, meaningful storytelling techniques?

    _____

    _____

    _____

    _____

    If "no," justify your answer. In other words, why is this information so compelling that your target audience will be innately interested?

    _____

    _____

    _____

    _____

GENERAL ACTIVITY 5.6: STYLE: EXPRESSING POINT-OF-VIEW

BACKGROUND: The same story can be told in many different ways. Style is the point-of-view the writer takes toward the subject. Writers may choose from a variety of styles: you may be playful, analytical, humorous, serious, angry, solemn, theatrical—the whole range of human emotions is available to scriptwriters.

Ideally, you will tell your story in a way that is uniquely you. A style you are comfortable with. A style you find interesting.

You express that style through everything that is seen or heard by viewers. This makes style more complex for the media writer than for print writers.

Media writers must think simultaneously about visual and verbal style. About sound effects and music. About transitions and special effects.

WHAT TO DO: In the space provided, list as many elements affecting the style of a media presentation as you can.

Visual Elements:	Audio & Verbal Elements:

SCRIPTWRITING WORKSHEET 9: MAKING STYLISTIC DECISIONS

WHAT TO DO: Answer the following questions with your own project in mind.

1. Describe the overall tone or point-of-view you would like to take toward the subject matter:

2. How will this attitude be communicated through visual cues?

_____

_____

_____

_____

3. How will this attitude be communicated through narration, dialogue, music, sound, etc.?

_____

_____

_____

_____

4. If you intend to mix contrasting styles (a comedic vignette within an otherwise serious piece), how will you ensure the two styles will function synergistically?

_____

_____

_____

_____

MINI-LESSON: CONCEPT DEVELOPMENT

Although the term concept is ambiguous, it is the best I know to express this final phase of the Rehearsal process. Here are several definitions—each capturing important elements of a strong creative concept:

- A single idea or premise which shapes style, format, content and structure into a unified, aesthetically pleasing whole.

- The creative vehicle for conveying content.

- A storytelling theme used to provide a warm, human touch to the cold facts which constitute the content.

- The scriptwriter's answer to the question: "what if?"

Once a concept is set, parameters for aesthetic and production considerations are established. As the first definition implies, it is the sum of all the aesthetic decisions the media writer makes—and yet it is more.

Think of it this way: imagine your "dream house"—the home you'd build or buy if money were no object. The elements of your dream house could be described this way:

Format—The generic type of home you'd build: colonial, Tudor, ranch, contemporary, farm house, etc.

Structure—The layout of rooms in your home: will it have one floor, two, or several? Where will living room, den and kitchen be located? How will you move from room to room?

Style—The overall "feeling" you'd want guests to experience in your home. Will it be elegant and formal, or warm and casual? This influences the materials chosen for the structure: stucco and stone versus natural wood and glass.

Concept—After describing these elements to an architect, he or she develops a design that reflects your input. Ideally, that design blends format, structure and style in a way that makes for a pleasing, satisfying whole.

SCRIPTWRITING WORKSHEET 10: DREAM A LITTLE

WHAT TO DO: Before getting practical—dream a little. Imagine if you had unlimited resources, time and talent to produce your own program. No limitations. No clients with negative attitudes. What would you do?

This is your time for the "daydreaming part." Describe the program you would like to write under ideal conditions with no limitations. It will be the most effective way to communicate the content to your target audience:

MINI-LESSON: CONCEPT EVALUATION MATRIX

Students of the creative writing process have noted how seemingly opposite states of mind are necessary to produce a creative product.

It's often called a Janusian process—after the Roman god of doorways and beginnings, Janus. His multiple faces look simultaneously in opposite directions.

Peter Elbow describes the Janusian dilemma all writers face: "Writing calls on two skills that are so different they usually conflict with each other: creating and criticizing."

So far, the Rehearsal stage of scriptwriting has focused on creative possibilities—imagining the various forms a script might take.

As the writer's vision yields specific concepts, it is time to "face the opposite direction" and *evaluate* these concepts with a critical, judgmental eye.

The *Concept Evaluation Matrix* is one tool for conducting this critical evaluation.

The best concepts satisfy the criteria inherent in all these elements.

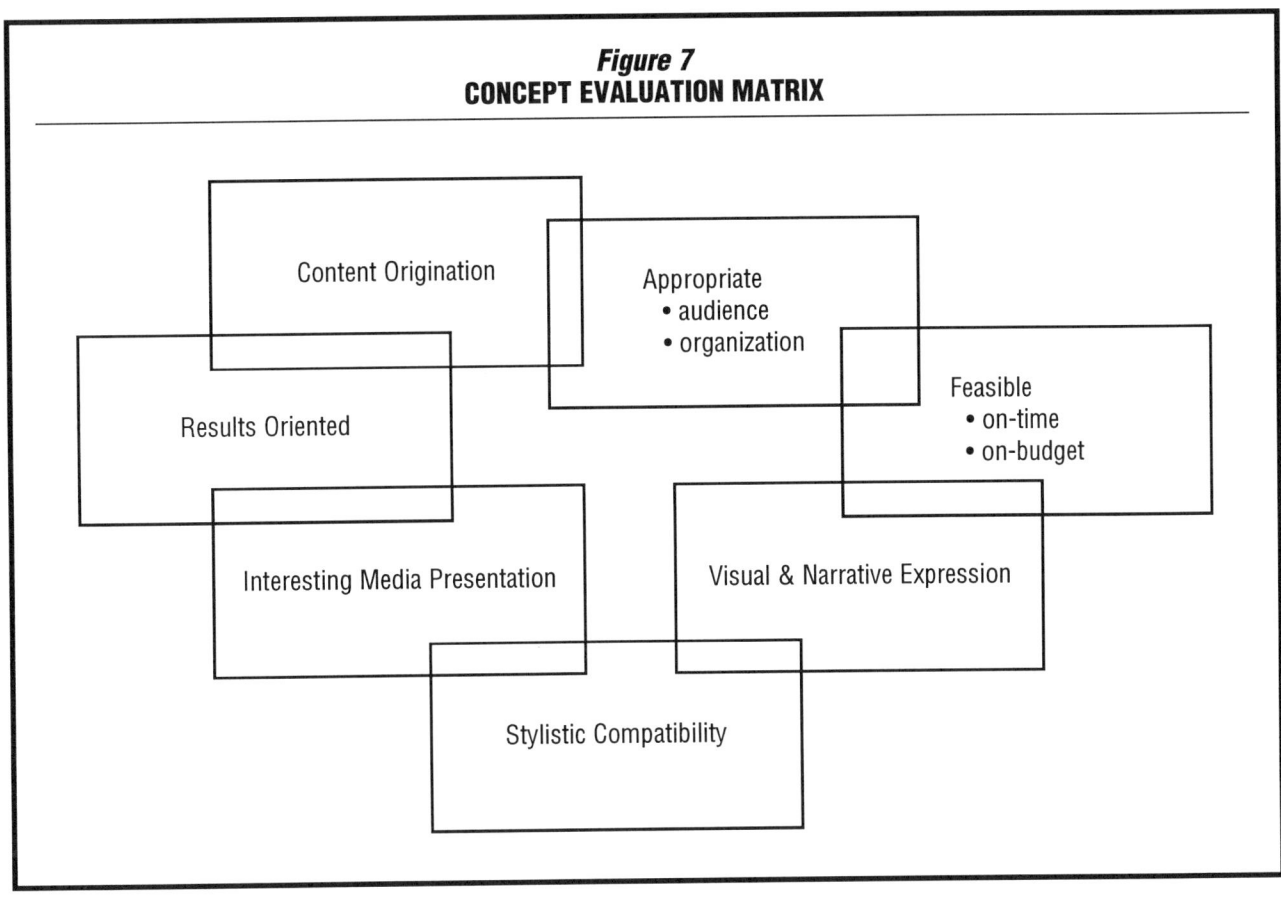

Figure 7
CONCEPT EVALUATION MATRIX

- Content Origination: Does the concept spring from careful consideration of subject matter; or, is it arbitrarily imposed on the subject? Strong creative concepts have a sense of inevitability that comes from letting content dictate form.

- Appropriateness: Your concept should be appropriate for the organization and specific target audience.

- Feasibility: If an otherwise good concept cannot be properly executed on time and on budget—you must refine the concept or explore alternatives.

- Visual & Narrative Expression: Your concept should encourage a synergistic use of the chosen medium's capabilities. (Good audio scripts often stimulate vivid visual imagination.)

- Stylistic Compatibility: All elements of your concept should be organically integrated. Does everything come together to form an aesthetically pleasing whole?

- Interesting Media Presentation: Your concept should make for an intrinsically interesting, memorable media program. There are no "boring subjects;" only "boring writing."

- Results Oriented: Return to your objectives and honestly determine whether this concept achieves results that match the client's expectations.

SCRIPTWRITING WORKSHEET 11: APPLYING THE MATRIX TO YOUR CONCEPT

WHAT TO DO: You've considered your program's format, structure and style. Next, work at imagining the content in your head as a fully produced viewing experience. Try to "see" pictures that will appear on screen and "hear" narration, dialogue and sound.

Imagine the "chronological sequence of events" that will comprise the viewing or listening experience.

Evaluate your concept by answering the questions relating to the Concept Development Matrix.

1. Briefly describe the concept in your own words:

    _____

    _____

    _____

    _____

    _____

2. Now critically evaluate your concept by checking the appropriate item for each question.
    A. Evaluate how well the concept functions as a "spine" to unify format, style and structure in terms of the program *content*.
    _____ Unsatisfactory
    _____ Marginal
    _____ Satisfactory
    _____ Outstanding

    B. Evaluate how appropriate the concept is for the target audience.
    _____ Unsatisfactory
    _____ Marginal
    _____ Satisfactory
    _____ Outstanding

    C. Evaluate how appropriate the concept is for the company or organization.
    _____ Unsatisfactory
    _____ Marginal
    _____ Satisfactory
    _____ Outstanding

    D. Evaluate the concept in terms of feasibility.

Production Time:	*Budget & Resources*
_____ Unsatisfactory	_____ Unsatisfactory
_____ Marginal	_____ Marginal
_____ Satisfactory	_____ Satisfactory
_____ Outstanding	_____ Outstanding

E. Evaluate the concept's potential for synergistic visual and narrative expression.

    ____ Unsatisfactory
    ____ Marginal
    ____ Satisfactory
    ____ Outstanding

F. Evaluate how well major program segments and formats will work together stylistically.

    ____ Unsatisfactory
    ____ Marginal
    ____ Satisfactory
    ____ Outstanding

G. Evaluate how effectively the concept fulfills client expectations. Is it results-oriented, rooted in careful consideration of audience, viewing environment and objectives?

    ____ Unsatisfactory
    ____ Marginal
    ____ Satisfactory
    ____ Outstanding

3. Have you identified any significant flaws in your concept?

               ____ Yes   ____ No

If "yes..."

• Either the strengths of the concept must outweigh potential liabilities, or...
• You must adjust the concept accordingly, or...
• You must go back to the "drawing-board" and develop a new concept.

GENERAL ACTIVITY 5.7: THE MEDIA TREATMENT

BACKGROUND: Just as architects make preliminary sketches to convey the essence of the finished building before committing to blue prints, media treatments function as narrative "sketches" the writer develops prior to drafting a detailed shooting script.

        The media treatment expresses the writer's emerging vision of the viewing experience in simple narrative prose. To write a treatment, simply transcribe the sights and sounds imagined during rehearsal.

WHAT TO DO: The treatment is the one writing product you produce at the end of the Rehearsal stage to share with producer, client, content expert and director.

        Brainstorm the *functions* a media treatment serves, its value at this stage in the script development process and list in the space provided.

_____

_____

_____

_____

SCRIPTWRITING WORKSHEET 12
ARE YOU READY TO WRITE A TREATMENT?

WHAT TO DO: Answering the following questions will tell you if you're prepared to write a treatment—a "sketch" of your vision of the ultimate viewing experience in chronological sequence.

1. Can you "see" and "hear" the program unfold as a chronological sequence of events in your mind?

    ____ Yes   ____ No

    If "No," go back over previous scriptwriting worksheets to see if you can stimulate mental sights and sounds. Once you answer "yes," proceed to the remaining questions...

2. Describe how the program will open. Use words that describe "sights" and "sounds" the viewer will see and hear.

    _____

    _____

    _____

    _____

3. How does this opening "hook" the target audience? If you're uncertain, review the Audience Profile and Communication Environment descriptions.

    _____

    _____

    _____

    _____

    _____

4. How does your opening answer the question: "What's in it for me?"

    _____

    _____

    _____

    _____

    _____

5. Write out your "vision" of the Body of the program. (It will probably take several pages, so use additional sheets of paper.) Use words that describe "sights" and "sounds." Focus on how the chronological sequence of events unfold on the screen. Don't get too detailed. Summarize key content.

_____

_____

_____

_____

_____

_____

_____

_____

6. Then, answer the following questions about the description of the program's body:

A. Have you identified the primary visual images?

　　　　　　　　　____ Yes　　____ No

B. Have you identified the primary on and off-screen participants?

　　　　　　　　　____ Yes　　____ No

C. Have you described the primary locations and the action which occurs in them?

　　　　　　　　　____ Yes　　____ No

D. Have you described key transitions?

　　　　　　　　　____ Yes　　____ No

E. Have you described use of music, titles and supers, special effects, computer animation or other unusual techniques that effect production requirements?

　　　　　　　　　____ Yes　　____ No

F. Have you communicated a sense of the narrative and visual style?

　　　　　　　　　____ Yes　　____ No

G. Did you communicate a sense of the "big" scenes and what will make them the most memorable moments of the program?

　　　　　　　　　____ Yes　　____ No

H. Could the client read your description and visualize how the program will unfold on the screen?

_____ Yes _____ No

I. Could a producer or director use your treatment to address issues relating to production requirements, logistics, talent, editing and budgeting?

_____ Yes _____ No

An answer of "No" to any of these questions may indicate your treatment is not fully developed. Go back and flesh out those areas that lack specifics.

7. Finally, describe how the program concludes. Again, use words that relate to the "sights" and "sounds" of the viewing or listening experience.

_____

_____

_____

_____

_____

_____

8. Does this conclusion provide a sense of completion?

_____ Yes _____ No

9. Does the conclusion end on a high note—giving viewers more than a simple repetition of key points?

_____ Yes _____ No

10. If action is required on the part of the audience, is it clear what they are supposed to do following the program?

_____ Yes _____ No

11. Have you provided a "kicker"—something to leave your audience with a sense of satisfaction at the end?

_____ Yes _____ No

An answer of "no" to any of these questions may signal your program simply "stops". Like a sales presentation, good media programs require a powerful closing.

Go back and work out a closing that drives your message home forcefully. It need not be long, but it must have a strong conclusion that is conveyed with impact!

Figure 8
SAMPLE: MEDIA TREATMENT

Opening Teaser

We fade up on the entrance to the Consumer Center. The shot features the general store display, populated by characters in period costume. The storekeeper banters with a woman and her two young children. The woman is "stocking her larder" for the month (the kids have only penny-candy on their minds). Talk is of the weather, crops and "when the new school marm's due to arrive."

As the lady runs down her shopping list, she asks to look at a "box of new Post Cereal." She peruses the package, then asks the storekeeper about its nutritional value or wholesomeness. . .

. . .at that moment, the dramatic action freezes, as the actors form a tableau. The Narrator (possibly a woman) enters frame and addresses camera.

"Consumers have always had questions about the products we make. As long ago as 1925, two home economists were hired by the company to form an educational department. They provided nutrition information about Post cereals and Postum beverages. Today, that department is known as the General Foods Consumer Center."

On this last line, the camera pans to the wall with contemporary "Consumer Center" graphics. Music and actuality audio punctuate a fast-paced montage of Consumer Center activities: pies going into a test kitchen oven; a photographer lighting a main dish still life; a high-speed word processing printer banging out a consumer response letter; a group of division and agency people are seen during an intense taste-testing.

Interwoven with these glimpses of Consumer Center activities is additional voice-over copy. The Narrator reinforces the pictorial impression that the Consumer Center involves many diverse activities. "All these activities mirror General Foods' responsiveness to consumer needs and concerns."

The narration establishes that in this program "we'll see and hear how each area of the Consumer Center advocates the interests of our consumers in all aspects of General Foods business."

This opening montage comes to an end with the program title—then fades momentarily to black. . .

MINI-LESSON: GUIDELINES FOR WRITING TREATMENTS

The good news is that by completing Scriptwriting Worksheet 12, you've probably created a rough first draft of your treatment.

Before polishing to make it "client ready," read through the Sample Treatment. Then use these Guidelines for Writing Treatments and polish your treatment:

1. Write the treatment according to the chronological sequence of events you see unfolding on the screen—what happens first, second and so on.

2. Describe the location and principle on-screen participants for each major scene.

3. Describe sights and sounds viewers will see and hear.

4. Indicate major transitions.

5. Describe important sets, cutaway footage, graphics, computer or special effects and titles.

6. Don't overwrite. The treatment is a general description of how the program will unfold in prose form. Keep it simple. Capture the essence of your creative concept.

MINI-LESSON: COMPLETE PROJECT PROPOSAL

The conclusion of the Assimilation and Rehearsal stage represents a major milestone in the scriptwriting process. In addition to your Research Agenda, you have created four writing products:

- Audience Profile

- Program Objectives

- Content Outline

- Media Treatment

Taken together, these documents should provide everyone involved in the project sufficient information to determine if your analysis of the communication/training problem and your proposed media solution is on-target.

If your media treatment is complete and descriptive, a preliminary budget and shooting schedule can be estimated. Providing a budget and schedule along with these other documents provides a Complete Project Proposal.

Decision-makers have all the input needed to approve the project. If there are problems with your approach, now is the time to find out—before drafting a complete shooting script.

If your overall approach is approved, you proceed to the Drafting stage confident you are on the right track. You have successfully completed the most difficult and crucial part of the writer's task: up-front needs analysis and specific recommendations.

To paraphrase William Goldman, everything should be "clear in your head." Comfortable with the story you're telling, now you can "go like hell!"

Drafting the Shooting Script

(The Scriptwriter's Handbook, pages 121–138)

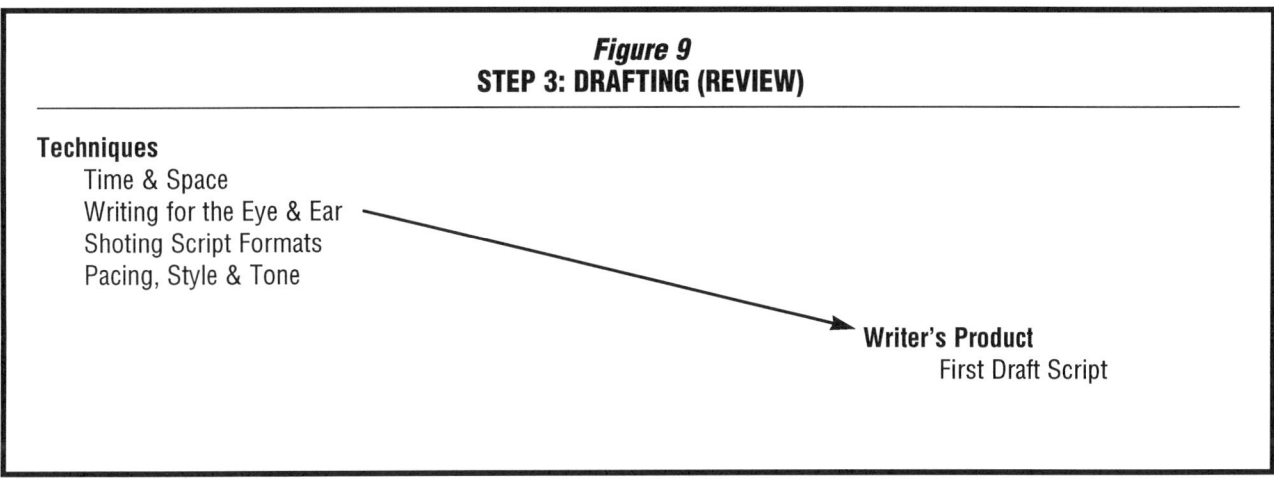

Figure 9
STEP 3: DRAFTING (REVIEW)

Techniques
   Time & Space
   Writing for the Eye & Ear
   Shoting Script Formats
   Pacing, Style & Tone

Writer's Product
   First Draft Script

REVIEW ACTIVITY

WHAT TO DO: Answer the following questions. Refer to the appropriate chapters in *The Scriptwriter's Handbook* if necessary.

1. Identify at least three ways in which a shooting script goes beyond the media treatment:

   _____

   _____

   _____

2. To describe the viewing experience, or chronological sequence of events, and the relationship between sight and sound cues, the writer uses a special vocabulary known as:

   _____

   _____

3. Two standard shooting script formats are:

_____

_____

4. Aesthetician Susanne Langer describes two types of symbol systems:

Language communicates through "a linear, discrete successive order" governed by laws of syntax. Langer calls this a:

_____ symbol

Visual symbol systems, such as painting or sculpture, communicate their meaning simultaneously. Langer calls this a:

_____ symbol

Which symbol system does the media writer employ? _____

5. When you want absolute certainty the client's perception of visual images matches your intent, the best technique is to:

_____

_____

GENERAL ACTIVITY 6.1: ARTIST VS. JUDGE

BACKGROUND: One of today's master writing teachers, Lucy McCormick Calkins, often describes drafting as a mental teeter-totter: the writer goes back and forth from "passion hot to critic cold" as the draft emerges.

WHAT TO DO: Respond to the dual notions of the "artist" vs. the "critic or judge". What qualities do you associate with the artistic personality? What about the judgmental personality? Jot down as many associations as come to mind—your "gut reactions" to the words. Go for as many associations as you can generate.

Characteristics of the artistic personality	Characteristics of the critic or judgmental personality
_____	_____
_____	_____
_____	_____
_____	_____
_____	_____

1. Which personality are you most comfortable with?

   _____

   _____

2. Which personality do you think is most important to the drafting process?

   _____

   _____

In getting a first draft on paper, writers are often advised to keep words and sentences flowing as freely as possible: "free writing," Peter Elbow calls it. As the name implies, a draft is a preliminary or tentative version. Striving for too much perfection at this stage can short-circuit the normal writing process.

Drafting is not the time to pause over spelling or even grammatical usage. The challenge is to make certain your "passion hot" enthusiasm is not cooled by too much of the critic's "cold water." Too harsh a judgmental attitude in the drafting phase leads to that dreaded condition: writer's block.

Script Formats

In addition to these normal writing concerns, some beginning scriptwriters allow the page layout and production terminology used in media writing to intimidate them—needlessly complicating the free flowing feel of the drafting process.

Before moving on, let's spend some time analyzing shooting script formats. . .

WRITING PRODUCT 5:
TWO COMMON SHOOTING SCRIPT FORMATS

ANALYSIS: In reality, script page formats are relatively simple. You use either a standard two column video or slide show format (Figure 10); or, a film style format that does not require side by side columns (Figure 11).

Once the appropriate format is entered into a word processing program as a template, you'll find it soon becomes second nature. (There are even specific video and film script word processing software programs to facilitate use of these script formats.)

But never allow a page format or production terminology to impede the "passion hot" phase of drafting.

Your shooting script is simply a more detailed, complete version of the treatment. Focus on capturing the "sights and sounds" of the program that has been emerging in your mind's eye.

The following activities and mini-lessons are designed to help novice scriptwriters overcome "shooting script format phobia," concentrating instead on constructing the chronological sequence of events of their media viewing experience.

63

Figure 10
SAMPLE: SHOOTING SCRIPT FORMAT I
(2 Column Video/Slide Show Page Layout)

VIDEO	AUDIO
LS—Wide angle view of model office. Narrator moves towards TRIPS terminal.	**NARRATOR:** OUR NEW TRAVEL SERVICE OFFICE— MODERN, COMFORTABLE, SPACIOUS. THE OFFICE ITSELF SAYS "PRESTIGE, INTEGRITY, SECURITY AND SERVICE."
ZOOM in to MS of Narrator and terminal.	THIS IS THE TRIPS TERMINAL, AND AS YOU CAN SEE, IT'S RIGHT AT HOME IN OUR NEW ENVIRONMENT.
CU—On Narrator.	BUT WHAT IS TRIPS? TRIPS IS A MULTI-ACCESS RETAIL RESERVATIONS, ACCOUNTING AND COMMUNICATIONS SYSTEM. . . AND TO CALL IT REVOLUTIONARY IS AN UNDERSTATEMENT. THE TRIPS COMPUTER SYSTEM PUTS THE WHOLE WORLD OF TRAVEL INFORMATION *LITERALLY* AT YOUR FINGERTIPS.
ECU—Of hands on terminal keyboard.	IT'S AS SIMPLE AS A TYPEWRITER. . . AND AS NEW AS TOMORROW.
ECU—On CRT screen displaying information.	IT'S A NEW WAY OF HANDLING INFORMATION. . .
Info on CRT screen changes rapidly two or three times. Screen now shows the artwork graphic of globe with animated network.	ALL KINDS OF INFORMATION. IT'S A NEW METHOD TO ENHANCE OUR WORLD-WIDE DISTRIBUTION NETWORK. . . OUR WHOLE MARKETING EFFORT.
MS—On Narrator and terminal.	IT'S A NEW TECHNIQUE TO EXPAND OUR CUSTOMER SERVICE CAPABILITIES. TRIPS MAKES AVAILABLE, FOR THE FIRST TIME ANYWHERE, *ALL* OF OUR TRAVEL RESOURCES ON A MULTI-ACCESS TERMINAL:
Cut to MS on jet liner taking off.	. . . . . . AIRLINES . . . . . .
Cut to MS on exterior of famous hotel.	. . . . . . HOTELS . . . . . .
Cut to MS of tour bus or group tour.	. . . . . . TOURS . . . . . .
Cut to MS of car rental area in airport terminal.	. . . . . . CAR RENTALS . . . . . .
ECU—On terminal with display.	. . . . . . OTHER TRS SYSTEMS . . . . . .
MS—On Narrator by terminal.	EVERYTHING—RIGHT HERE ON THIS ONE SCREEN.

Source: From "Trips: Your Selling and Servicing Partner," written by Allen Neil, directed by James G. Libby, produced by Video Marketing Group for American Express Travel Services. Used by permission.

Figure 11
SAMPLE: SHOOTING SCRIPT FORMAT II
(Film or Motion Picture Page Layout)

---

1. INT. WIDE ANGLE SHOT OF TRAVEL OFFICE. NARRATOR ENTERS AND MOVES TOWARD TRIPS TERMINAL.

   NARRATOR
   (Addressing camera.) Our new travel Service Office—modern, comfortable, spacious. The office itself says "prestige, integrity, security and service."

2. ZOOM IN TO TWO-SHOT OF NARRATOR AND TERMINAL.

   NARRATOR
   This is the TRIPS terminal. And, as you can see, it's right at home in our new envionment.

3. CLOSE-UP ON NARRATOR.

   NARRATOR
   But what is TRIPS? TRIPS is a multi-access retail reservations, accounting and communications system. . . and to call it revolutionary is an understatement. The TRIPS computer system puts the whole world of travel information *literally* at your fingertips.

4. EXTREME CLOSE-UP OF HANDS OPERATING KEYBOARD TERMINAL.

   NARRATOR
   It's as simple as a typewriter. . . and as new as tomorrow.

5. EXTREME CLOSE-UP ON CRT SCREEN DISPLAYING INFORMATION.

   NARRATOR
   It's a new way of handling information. . .

6. INFO ON CRT SCREEN CHANGES RAPIDLY TWO OR THREE TIMES.

   NARRATOR
   all kinds of information. It's a new method to enhance our world-wide distribution network. . .

7. MEDIUM SHOT ON NARRATOR AND TERMINAL.

   NARRATOR
   It's a new technique to expand our customer service capabilities. TRIPS makes available, for the first time anywhere, all of our travel resources on a multi-access terminal:

8. EXT. CLOSE-UP SHOT OF JET LINER TAKING OFF.

   NARRATOR
   Airlines. . .

9. EXT. MEDIUM SHOT OF FAMOUS HOTEL ENTRANCE.

   NARRATOR
   Hotels. . .

10. EXT. MEDIUM SHOT OF TOUR BUS OR TOUR GROUP.

    NARRATOR
    Tours. . .

11. EXT. MEDIUM SHOT OF CAR RENTAL AREA IN AIRPORT TERMINAL.

    NARRATOR
    Car rentals. . .

12. INT. EXTREME CLOSE-UP ON TERMINAL WITH DISPLAY.

    NARRATOR
    Other TRS systems. . .

13. INT. MEDIUM SHOT OF NARRATOR BY TERMINAL.

    NARRATOR
    Everything—right here on this one screen.

Source: From "Trips: Your Selling and Servicing Partner," written by Allen Neil, directed by James G. Libby, produced by Video Marketing Group for American Express Travel Services. Used by permission.

GENERAL ACTIVITY 6.2: COMPARING SHOOTING SCRIPT FORMATS

WHAT TO DO: After reading the two sample scripts, answer the following questions:

1. Which script format do you think is easier for a client, content expert or others not used to reading scripts to visualize how the program will flow as a viewing experience?

    _____ Two-Column Video   _____ Motion Picture Format

2. Beginning scriptwriters often make the mistake of writing narration or dialogue first—then the pictures. Which script format do you think encourages this approach?

    _____ Two-Column Video   _____ Motion Picture Format

3. Which script format do you think most precisely shows the exact relationship between audio and visual cues?

    _____ Two-Column Video   _____ Motion Picture Format

4. From a word-processing standpoint, which format do you think is most user-friendly?

    _____ Two-Column Video   _____ Motion Picture Format

GENERAL ACTIVITY 6.3: THE 60-SECOND BENCHMARK

BACKGROUND: Except for audio and portions of multi-media scripts, all media presentations are a continuous evolution of spatial relationships between camera and subject. . .

   . . .coordinated with a sequence of audio events. The rate at which those spatial relationships and audio events change is known as pacing.

   Whether using the two-column video script or the film script format, one full page generally equals about one minute of screen time.

   You can use this rule of thumb to assess both overall running time and the general pacing within the program.

WHAT TO DO: If pacing is the rate at which visual and auditory events change—list those sight and sound elements available to the scriptwriter for changing the pace. What visual and auditory tools do you have to effect change. Which elements of change are within your control as writer?

Visual Elements	Auditory Elements
_____	_____
_____	_____
_____	_____
_____	_____
_____	_____
_____	_____

Now, answer these questions, keeping the sixty-second rule-of-thumb in mind:

1. Writing using the dual column format, you notice you have a full page of narration and a single shot description. What does this tell you about your pacing?

    _____

    _____

    _____

    _____

2. You are on page 8 of a script that is ten minutes long. Where should you be in terms of the overall arc of the program?

    _____

    _____

    _____

    _____

3. What if you still have significant content to communicate?

    _____

    _____

    _____

    _____

4. What is the difference in pacing between a shot in which the screen is static and a shot in which the screen action is continuously changing?

    _____

    _____

    _____

    _____

CHAPTER 7

Imaginative Writing for the Eye and Ear

(The Scriptwriter's Handbook, pages 139–193)

REVIEW ACTIVITY

WHAT TO DO: Answer the following questions. Refer to the appropriate chapters in *The Scriptwriter's Handbook* if necessary.

1. Identify three visualization problems beginning media writers sometimes experience:

   _____

   _____

   _____

2. To overcome these problems, identify three "Guidelines for Effective Visualization."

   _____

   _____

   _____

3. Many camera directions media writers use in a script describe the changing relationship between the _____ and the _____.

4. Describe the difference between these common visual transitions used in a variety of media:
   a) Fade Up; or, Fade to Black
   b) Dissolve

   _____

   _____

   _____

c) Dissolve

d) Wipe

_____

_____

_____

5. According to Murray, what is the element of a story that "carries its emotional force?"

_____

_____

_____

6. Read over the following descriptions of media program subjects or topics within a media program. Then, decide whether the subject is best suited to a professional narrator or a company spokesperson. Enter "P" for Professional Narrator; "CS" for Company Spokesperson:

_____ Explanation of why your company has been acquired by another.

_____ Detailed description of company benefit plans.

_____ Expression of company's commitment to provide competitive benefits.

_____ Explanation of how new Food & Drug Administration (FDA) guidelines effect a pharmaceutical company's Physician Speakers Program.

_____ Statement of that pharmaceutical company's commitment to abide by FDA Guidelines.

_____ Training program on principles of credit management.

7. Narration is the "workhorse" of corporate and documentary media presentations. What are four general categories of narrative copy identified in Chapter 8 of *The Scriptwriter's Handbook*?

_____

_____

_____

_____

8. What is the primary function of music in a media production?

_____

_____

_____

9. In the early days of radio, writers challenged their listening audiences to imagine the action of a radio drama in the mind's eye. This prompted radio writers to refer to their medium as _____ of the imagination.

MINI-LESSON: VISUAL SHOOTING SCRIPT TERMINOLOGY

As mentioned, Peter Elbow encourages what he calls "free writing: First, write freely and uncritically so that you can generate as many words and ideas as possible without worrying whether they are good," he says.

Don't let the language of production terminology impede this process. Ninety percent of the time, you'll use the same few terms over and over and over again:

TYPICAL VISUAL PRODUCTION TERMINOLOGY:
The most frequently used terms describing what's happening on the screen are:

Long Shot (LS)
Medium Shot (MS)
Close Up (CU)
Extreme Close Up (ECU)

These four terms describe the relative **distance** between the camera and the subject. You'll use these terms a good 75 to 80 percent of the time.

In addition, you'll sometimes want to call for camera movement in relation to the subject. Here, too, six terms almost always suffice:

Pan Right
Pan Left

Horizontal movement of the camera left or right across the subject.

Tilt Up
Tilt Down

Vertical camera movement up or down the subject.

Zoom In
Zoom Out

Bringing the image closer. . .
. . .or farther away by adjusting the camera lens.

These few terms will serve almost all your needs for describing the relationship between the camera and subject.

TRANSITIONS

When it comes to transitions from one scene to the next, the most common terms are:

CUT TO:

The "CUT" is an instantaneous change between two shots or images. The final frame of *Scene A* is followed immediately by the first frame of *Scene B*.

NOTE: Although you can use a CUT to go from one scene to the next, it doesn't mean every CUT is a transition. The simple CUT from one shot to the next or one image to another is the typical method of going from shot to shot. Transitions imply a change in locale or time.

DISSOLVE TO:

In a DISSOLVE, the tail end of *Scene A* FADES OUT as the first images of *Scene B* simultaneously FADE IN. For a few seconds, the two images *overlap*—creating a fluid transition.

The DISSOLVE is almost always used to signal changes in time. DISSOLVES are also useful in setting mood and slowing the visual pace.

If you're drafting your first script, stick to these two transitions between scenes. Concentrate on describing the visual material you picture in your mind's eye.

DESCRIBING ON-SCREEN ACTION

Sometimes, you'll use the visual column to describe ACTION taking place within the frame. For example:

VIDEO

Action begins as actor portrays Joel Cheek. Cheek moves about in office with turn-of-the-century memorabilia. He uses props and photo album to illustrate his story.

MS on Cheek as he moves to saddle-bags slung over chair.

INSERT close-ups as he pulls coffee bean samples from the bag.

FOLLOW ACTION as he moves to copper kettle and empties samples into kettle.

GENERAL ACTIVITY 7.1: VISUAL SHOOTING SCRIPT TERMINOLOGY

WHAT TO DO: The following activity will give you practice using this scriptwriting language...

BACKGROUND: *How Much Is Necessary?*

Beginning scriptwriters often worry over how much detail to use in describing visuals. There are no specific rules. Subject matter influences this decision.

If you are writing a training program about highly technical subject matter, call out specific shots on equipment or graphics as necessary. If writing about a medical procedure, for example, describe the visual action step-by-step and shot-by-shot to match narrative copy.

By contrast, if scripting a dramatization of an employment interview—leave blocking and camera shots to the director's discretion. Simply write a master scene.

At some key moment—you may wish to insert a **close-up** to highlight facial expression or INSERT an ECU on notes the interviewer is taking. Otherwise, leave camera and editing decisions to the director.

GENERAL ACTIVITY 7.2: WRITING CAMERA DIRECTIONS

BACKGROUND: If you've never written camera directions before, this exercise gives you practice.

WHAT TO DO: The illustration below depicts the view from a writer's woodland retreat. (The antique object on the table is a manual typewriter. No batteries needed!) Read the description of "where the shot begins" and "where the shot ends." Then, write an appropriate camera direction in the space to the right of the illustrations. Refer to the list of common camera directions if you find them helpful.

Where shot begins: the camera includes only the stream outside the window. . .
Where shot ends: a complete view of the desk and portraits on wall.

Write an appropriate description of the shot and movement of camera (or lens) to arrive at the ending shot.

Where shot begins: the camera is focused on the portrait of Charles Dickens to the right of the window.
Where shot ends: the camera moves to focus on the portrait of Emily Dickinson to the left of the window.

Write an appropriate description of the shot and movement of camera (or lens) to arrive at the ending shot.

Where shot begins: the camera includes only the stream outside the window. . .
Where shot ends: shot shows only the typewriter.

Write an appropriate description of the shot and movement of the camera (or lens) to arrive at the ending shot.

Where shot begins: camera shows entire scene. . .
Where shot ends: a shot showing only portrait of Emily Dickinson left of the window.

Write an appropriate description of the shot and movement of the camera (or lens) to arrive at the ending shot.

SCRIPTWRITING WORKSHEET 13: VISUALS IN YOUR SCRIPT

WHAT TO DO: Before proceeding, answer the following questions about the visual material of your program:

1. Check the box which best describes the primary type of visual material you envision for your program:

    ____ location action footage

    ____ studio setting

    ____ still photos or graphics

    ____ animated graphics

    ____ a combination
    Describe this mix:

    _____

    _____

2. Describe the primary function of your footage, visuals, graphics, photos and/or sets—i.e., Do they serve a specific purpose in communicating content, or do they function more to set a mood or tone? You may, of course, use both types in your program.

    _____

    _____

3. Describe the visual style or look you are aiming for in your program.

    _____

    _____

4. In a previous worksheet (Scriptwriting Worksheet 5, item 5), you identified the "big moments" of your program. These are the key points you want to be most memorable. Can you think of visually arresting, memorable images that correspond to these big moments? Describe below:

    _____

    _____

5. What script page layout do you wish to use?

    ____ Dual column video or slide format

    ____ Film script format

GENERAL ACTIVITY 7.3: WRITING FOR THE EAR

BACKGROUND: Narration is the workhorse of media scriptwriting. Usually, narrative copy falls into one of four categories:

- On-camera narration

- Off-camera narration (voice-over)

- Executive message/Content expert commentary

- Character narrations

In each case, a living, breathing human voice brings words on paper to life. The viewing audience reads nothing. They listen, instead, to human voices speaking.

WHAT TO DO: Brainstorm ways in which writing narration—words for other people to read as others listen—differs from writing words meant to be read by a reader on paper.

_____

_____

_____

_____

_____

_____

1. Given all these factors, what do you think is the "acid test" for your own narrative copy?

_____

_____

_____

_____

2. What are several ways of doing this?

_____

_____

_____

_____

GENERAL ACTIVITY 7.4: THE POWER OF VOICE

BACKGROUND: When writing copy for the executive or content expert to deliver on camera, the writer must consider the speaker's personality. In those cases, adopt the speaker's voice—not one of your own creation.

Finding an appropriate voice is also essential when writing character narrations—that is when information is conveyed through a monologue in which the narrator *assumes* the identity of a character. (Bringing a historical figure to life to recount the founding of a company is one example.)

"Voice," says writing coach Donald Murray, "gives the illusion of individual writer speaking to individual reader" (substitute "viewer").

Murray advises writers "to develop a range of voices" seeking one best suited to the needs of the project.

The following activity will help you develop voice...

WHAT TO DO: Do two rewrites of the following "voiceless" prose (taken from an executive speech) by selecting from the **menu** of voices listed below. Check two voices that are quite diverse—as well as voices you know well.

EXECUTIVE SPEECH TEXT

"Electronic communication and jet plane travel have made this world a much smaller place in the past twenty years. Ideas fly around the world in an instant. Cultural traits are rapidly exchanged and harmonized. Differences among people and among markets have become less pronounced. This trend will continue.

"That's why meetings like this are so important. Beyond offering the obvious benefits of getting to know one another, they provide a keener sense of how we can all cooperate more fully. And we'll have an opportunity to put that cooperation to work in the months ahead."

VOICE SELECTION MENU

____ **Dolly Parton**

____ **Norm or Cliff (from Cheers)**

____ **Bart, Homer or Marge Simpson**

____ **Murphy Brown**

____ **Miss Piggy or Kermit the Frog**

____ **Other** (Identify: _____)

____ **Bill Cosby**

____ **A Pirate King**

____ **A "Street Smart" Homeless Person**

____ **A "Jock" or Hayden Fox (from Coach)**

____ **A "Valley Girl" or Phoebe (from Friends)**

Identify the two different voices you will assume in rewriting the Executive Speech Text. In doing this activity, exaggerate your use of voice. The more distinctive you make it—the better.

Rewrite #1: Voice Selection: _____

Text:

_____

_____

_____

Rewrite #2: Voice Selection: _____

Text:

_____

_____

_____

ANALYSIS: In doing this exercise, you should have experienced how a change in "voice" influences vocabulary, sentence structure and length, and overall style and tone.

Although exaggerated, this same technique can be used to help you "lock in" on a conversational voice appropriate to a specific script or character.

WRITING PRODUCT 6: MUSIC & SOUND EFFECTS

BACKGROUND: Don't overlook the role of music and sound effects in your script. These auditory stimulants are another way of communicating content, setting mood and providing changes in pacing. Music and sound effects can:

- Establish mood

- Cue a transition

- Emphasize a point

- Support the pictures

- Play "against" the pictures

- Provide a rhythmic tempo for editing

- Communicate an emotion

- Provide a change of pace

- Surprise your viewers

78

Figure 12
SAMPLE SCRIPT EXCERPT
(Music & Sound Effects)

VIDEO	AUDIO
	SHIRLEY COOPER/INSTRUCTOR: MAKING THE TRANSITION FROM A LONG PERIOD OF UNEMPLOYMENT TO THE WORLD OF WORK IS THE KIND OF MAJOR CHANGE THAT CAN PROVE STRESSFUL
	WHAT DOES STRESS FEEL LIKE? SOME PEOPLE EXPERIENCE STRESS PHYSICALLY—SOME MENTALLY AND EMOTIONALLY. IN SOME WAYS, IT'S A LITTLE LIKE A ROLLER COASTER RIDE. . .
MOS FOOTAGE OF ROLLER COASTER RIDE. BEGIN WITH SEQUENCE OF ROLLER COASTER GOING SLOWLY TOWARD THE TOP.	**SOUND EFFX & MUSIC** (Mix of carnival music and sounds of roller coaster and riders.)
	SHIRLEY COOPER/INSTRUCTOR: FIRST, THERE'S THE ANTICIPATION OF THE SLOW, STEEP CLIMB UPWARD. . .
SLO-MO OF ROLLER COASTER REACHING THE PEAK. . .	THEN THERE'S THAT BRIEF MOMENT WHEN YOU SEEM SUSPENDED IN TIME AT THE VERY TOP—STOMACH FULL OF KNOTS.
THEN NORMAL ACTION AS IT DESCENDS. INTERCUT REACTIONS OF RIDERS.	AND THEN, THE EXCITEMENT OF FREE FALL—THE FORCE OF GRAVITY TAKES OVER.
	AND FINALLY, THE EXHILARATION OF MAKING IT SAFELY TO THE END OF THE RIDE.
CU ON SHIRLEY COOPER.	SOME OF THE STRESS YOU EXPERIENCE TRAVELING TO THE WORLD OF WORK MAY MAKE YOU FEEL LIKE YOU'RE ON A ROLLER COASTER.
INTERCUT MOS FOOTAGE OF ROLLER COASTER WITH ALMOST SUBLIMINAL SHOTS OF LAURA, EDUARDO AND JAMES SCOTT AS SEEN PREVIOUSLY	USUALLY, THE PERIODS *CLOSEST* TO THE ACTUAL CHANGE ARE THE MOST STRESSFUL, LIKE THAT FIRST DAY OF CLASS. . .
	THE FIRST INTERVIEW. . .
	THE FIRST DAY ON THE JOB.
	ANTICIPATING THE CHANGE IS LIKE GOING UP THE ROLLER COASTER—THE CLOSER YOU ARE TO THE MOMENT OF CHANGE—THE GREATER THE FEAR.

Source: From "The Choice is Yours,"™ written by William Van Nostran, directed by Walter Schoenknecht, created and produced by Karli & Associates and The Prudential-Audio Visual Communications Division. Used by permission.

ANALYSIS: Notice how the music and sound effects cue is linked directly to a visual event. This excerpt also illustrates why you should always write narration and sound with "pictures in mind".

The "emotional roller coaster" analogy is a way of making an abstract concept, such as stress, more vivid. Sight and sound elements work together, each contributing to a unified viewing experience.

MINI-LESSON: GUIDELINES FOR SCRIPTING AUDIO

The following guidelines are offered as a summary to writing narration, dialogue and communicating music and sound effects.

• Always script narration with pictures in mind. If using the dual column format, script audio and visuals together.

• Don't fall into the trap of thinking narration carries all the content. If it does, perhaps you're writing an audio script—not a sight and sound media presentation.

• When generating your first draft, go for as much free and uninhibited "passion hot" writing as possible. Don't let production terminology slow you down.

• Write the way people talk. Use colloquialisms and contractions.

• Remain aware of pacing. Use the 60-second/page rule as a guide.

• Challenge yourself to think of imaginative ways to use music and sound effects to change pacing and make content memorable.

Revising and Editing the Script

(The Scriptwriter's Handbook, pages 197–212)

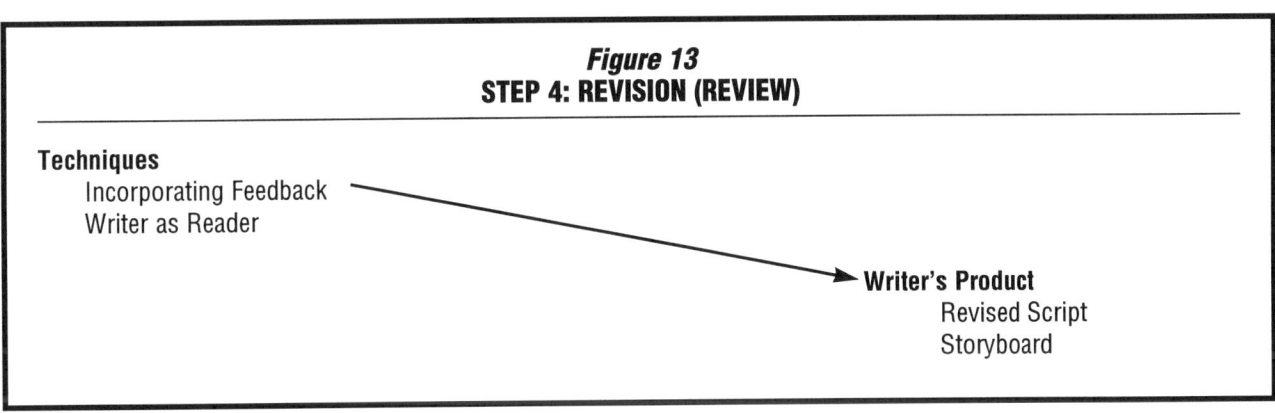

Figure 13
STEP 4: REVISION (REVIEW)

Techniques
Incorporating Feedback
Writer as Reader

Writer's Product
Revised Script
Storyboard

REVIEW ACTIVITY

1. "Revision" means: _____.

2. Only the writer relates to the shooting script as both _____ and _____.

3. In evaluating each individual script reader's feedback, media writers need to consider three related factors:

   _____ does it occur in the writing process?

   _____ does the feedback come from?

   _____ is the substance of the feedback?

4. When the client or Subject Matter Expert identifies a relevant, valid shortcoming in the first draft script, you should consider this a:

   _____ objection

5. What is the difference between a "Genuine" and a "Hopeless" objection?

_____

_____

6. When you first hear a genuine objection, you may totally agree or disagree. Name two other probable initial responses:

_____

_____

7. Why should you try to anticipate objections to a work in progress?

_____

_____

GENERAL ACTIVITY 8.1: "SEEING AGAIN"

BACKGROUND: The word "revision" often carries a pejorative connotation: rewriting means you didn't get it right the first time. More realistically, there are simply too many problems involved in writing a script to expect to solve them all in the first draft.

You can't focus your attention on everything at once. Often, it takes a first draft in order to identify just what needs to be done next.

Revision implies more than simply making changes—it literally means "to see again". If drafting is the time to be "passion hot", now is the time to don the judge's wig and take a critical look at the emerging viewing experience.

WHAT TO DO: Distinguish between "feedback" and "rejection" by entering your associations to the two words in the space provided. What's the difference between the two?

Feedback:	Rejection:

Difference between the two:

_____

_____

_____

ANALYSIS: As long as you write to meet the goals of others and satisfy their expectations, you'll need to include careful consideration of their feedback as part of the scripting process.

Seek Feedback Early

Avoid big surprises by soliciting feedback early in the process. This is the value of Content Outlines, Audience Profiles, Objectives and Treatments.

The most extensive feedback, however, generally occurs after review of the first draft script—because it is the most detailed treatment of the subject to date. Here are tips for handling feedback productively:

1. Always try to **anticipate** points in a script which may give one of your readers difficulty. Prepare your response in advance.

2. **Listen** carefully and fully to feedback. It's easy to "jump the gun" and begin defending before all feedback has been solicited. Take your time.

3. **Evaluate** the feedback.

SCRIPTWRITING WORKSHEET 14: RESPONDING TO YOUR ROUGH DRAFT

WHAT TO DO: Give yourself the pleasure of being the first to read your draft script critically. Before revisiting your script, think about what you experienced getting a rough draft down on paper (or in the word processor). Decide what you'd like to focus on in responding to the draft by answering the following questions.

1. First, what are the strengths of your rough draft—those things you feel best about accomplishing up to this point?

_____

_____

_____

_____

_____

2. Without even reading your rough draft, list those elements of the script you believe still need improving or more attention:

_____

_____

_____

Now—go ahead and read your draft script. Try to see *again* with fresh eyes. . .

3. Respond to what you have read. What do you consider the script's strong points?

_____

_____

_____

4. What things do you want to fix?

_____

_____

_____

5. Can you make these adjustments on your own—or will you need direction/input from the client or content expert?

_____ Yes   _____ No

SCRIPTWRITING WORKSHEET 15: REVISION CHECKLIST

WHAT TO DO: Before submitting your first draft shooting script for review and discussion, make sure you've made your first draft as strong as possible. Use the following Revision Checklist as a guide.

1._____ Have you read the script *aloud* and made changes accordingly?

2._____ Have you read the script once focusing solely on content?

3._____ Have you reviewed the draft in terms of the original objectives? Are you satisfied the draft achieves all objectives?

4._____ Have you read the script once focusing on the sight and sound synergy?

5._____ Have you read the script once focusing on your use of media production terminology?

6.____ Have you reviewed the script focusing on pacing, the timing of various segments and overall length?

7.____ Are you satisfied the script will result in an interesting viewing experience?

8.____ Has the production task remained feasible given time and budgetary parameters?

9.____ Has the draft shooting script remained faithful to the original treatment? If it differs, are you satisfied the new approach represents an improvement? Can you justify the new direction?

10.____ Is there anything about the shooting script that might need clarifying in a covering memo or in introductory remarks at the script review session? If so, plan how to handle this subject.

GENERAL ACTIVITY 8.2: PRESENTING THE FIRST DRAFT SCRIPT

BACKGROUND: Earlier, in General Activity 2.3, you identified those few select readers of your script. Figure 14 shows how clients, producers, content experts, directors and others view the script from different perspectives.

Each reader tends to focus on different aspects of the script. And, each reader brings various degrees of imaginative and visualization skills to this first reading.

WHAT TO DO: Describe the perspective and focus of each script reader in the space provided in each box.

Figure 14 **Script Reader Perspectives**	
Client:	**Producer:**
Content Expert:	**Director:**

WHAT TO DO: Consider the pros and cons of two common ways to present first draft shooting scripts by answering the following questions:

1. Sometimes, the draft shooting script is circulated among the principal script readers prior to a joint meeting so they all have time to respond individually and make notes on questions and concerns.

   List advantages of this approach:

   _____

   _____

   _____

   _____

   List *dis*advantages of this approach:

   _____

   _____

   _____

   _____

2. A second method is to call all principal script readers to a meeting where the writer presents the script by reading it aloud, getting a general response, then giving everyone an opportunity for individual, detailed review following the meeting.

   List advantages of this approach:

   _____

   _____

   _____

   _____

   List *dis*advantages of this approach:

   _____

   _____

   _____

   _____

GENERAL ACTIVITY 8.3: FEEDBACK SITUATIONS FOR ANALYSIS

WHAT TO DO: To help prepare for the multitude of situations scriptwriters often confront, answer the following case study questions.

1. The content expert offers feedback on the style of the script. What are some key considerations in analyzing his or her feedback?

    _____

    _____

    _____

    _____

2. The director offers feedback indicating concern over the feasibility of producing the script within budget or on schedule. What are key considerations in analyzing his or her feedback?

    _____

    _____

    _____

    _____

3. The client feels that the finished program, as written, will simply not fulfill his or her expectations. What are key considerations in analyzing his or her feedback?

    _____

    _____

    _____

    _____

4. The content expert feels that you have not fully understood one segment of the content. He or she has rewritten that segment. What are key considerations in analyzing this feedback and how should you respond?

    _____

    _____

    _____

    _____

5. Because of a company reorganization, you now have a *new* client who has not participated in any of the previous developmental work. The client is not at all satisfied with the creative approach. What are key considerations in analyzing this feedback?

_____

_____

_____

_____

MINI-LESSON: CATEGORIES OF OBJECTIONS

Not every objection means "no sale". Salespeople learn that objections are a normal part of the sales process.

To make the most productive response, salespeople classify objections and respond accordingly. It's a good technique for scriptwriters as well. Following are the three major categories of objections.

Hopeless Objection: An objection with the overall creative concept, its execution and the resulting draft script. Requires a complete rethinking of the project.

(This really should never happen if you've worked through the process with Objectives, Content Outlines, and Treatments and initiated the feedback process early.)

Minor Point Objection: You've done your homework, but the client feels compelled to find something wrong with the first draft.

Genuine Objection: A valid, legitimate problem or concern with some aspect of the first draft that usually requires fixing through revision. Initially, you may have one of several responses:

- Total Disagreement
- Total Agreement
- Uncertainty
- Confusion

GENERAL ACTIVITY 8.4: IDENTIFYING OBJECTIONS

WHAT TO DO: Listed below are several responses you might have to an objection raised in a script review. Write out the type of objection you think this response relates most closely to in the space provided:

1. You listen carefully to the feedback, but decide you should probe with follow-up questions to clarify. What type of objection are you most likely dealing with?

_____

_____

2. You decide you should counter the objection or concern, offering your perspective on why the revision is not appropriate. What type of objection are you most likely dealing with?

_____

_____

3. You buy time for more consideration of the objection or concern. What type of objection are you most likely dealing with?

_____

_____

4. What does this tell you about what types of objections are worth responding to?

_____

_____

SCRIPTWRITING WORKSHEET #15: ANALYZING FEEDBACK

WHAT TO DO: Every project brings unique revision requirements. Once you return from the initial review session, assess what needs to be accomplished in your rewrite. Use the following sheet to determine the extent and nature of revisions on your own project.

Content Related Revisions:

_____ Content errors need correcting

_____ Important content is missing

_____ Too much script time devoted to specific content points

_____ Content needs restructuring

_____ Content not sufficiently visualized

Narrative Related Revisions:

_____ Narration too "talky." Omit needless words.

_____ Narrative voice (or voices) convey inappropriate sense of tone.

_____ Narrative voice inconsistent in style and tone.

Visualization Related Revisions:

____ Content insufficiently visualized

____ Inappropriate visuals at times

____ Execution of visuals, graphics or sets go beyond what is feasible given budget or time parameters.

____ Client, content expert, producer or director having difficulty "picturing" graphics or settings from verbal description. (Often, a good solution is to storyboard a segment or do set design renderings.)

Conceptual Problems:

____ Script deviates significantly from treatment. (May be positive or negative.)

____ Client or others uncomfortable with concept now that it is fully developed.

____ Shooting script falls short in reaching the promise of the original concept as conveyed in treatment.

____ Other. Describe below

MINI-LESSON: REVISION STRATEGIES

In workshops, participants often overlook that the script writer is also one of those select group of script readers.

As a script reader, finding a sense of objectivity is your most difficult task. Whenever possible, try to schedule time to put a first draft aside for a few days so you can return to it with fresh "eyes".

Then, re-read the draft and ask yourself one simple, yet vital question: "Do I like it?" If not, you're also entitled to revise based on your own likes and dislikes as well as the feedback of others.

The following list of revision strategies are for you, the writer, to use whenever you feel they may help you make a good first draft better...

1. Change a section from one media format to another.

2. Rework a weak section—the ending, the open, a key point, an important transition, etc.

3. Reconsider tone or voice. Try a different voice and see if the new style is better.

4. Take a long script and make it shorter.

5. Experiment with different openings or closings.

6. Predict the viewer's questions. Then revise to ensure they are answered.

7. Read the script *aloud*—listening to how it sounds. Record your reading on an audio cassette. Play it back in the car while traveling. How does it sound?

8. Talk to someone about the topic. Then rewrite the draft without looking back at the previous versions. Compare the two. Is there something you like better in the new version? Insert it into the previous draft.

9. Read the script focusing on only one aspect, such as:

   • Narrative style and voice

   • Visualization

   • Structure and pacing

   • Formats

   • Transitions

   • Music and sound effects

   • Visual effects, etc.

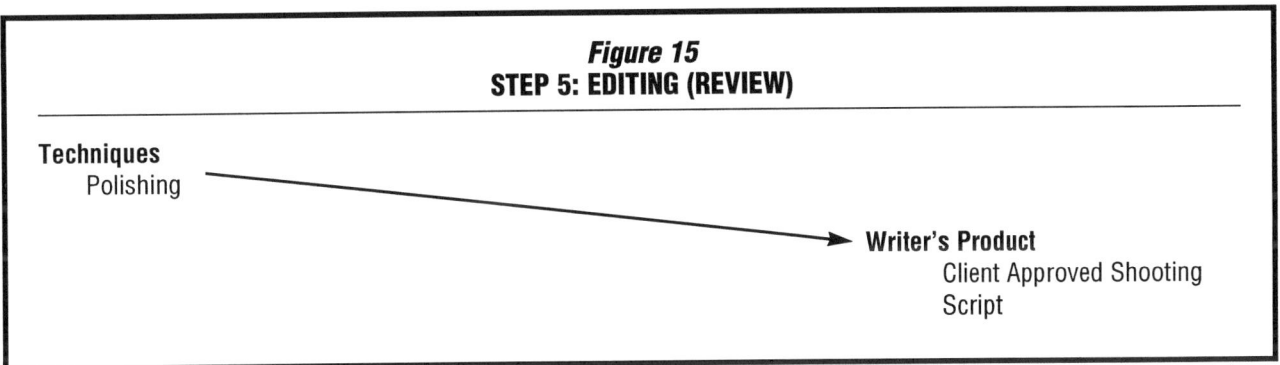

Figure 15
STEP 5: EDITING (REVIEW)

Techniques
Polishing

Writer's Product
Client Approved Shooting
Script

GENERAL ACTIVITY 8.5: EDITING THE SHOOTING SCRIPT

BACKGROUND: Looking at the scriptwriting process as a whole, it is always a matter of making choices between various options.

Early in the process, choices are about major issues:

   • What is the program about?

   • What formats are best suited to the content?

   • How do I want to treat the material creatively?

   • How do I structure the viewing experience?

As these early choices are made—the focus becomes narrower and narrower. In the editing phase, we really get down to fine points.

WHAT TO DO: What are the types of decisions and choices you should be making when you reach the third and fourth draft? Brainstorm the kinds of choices you think you should be focusing on at this stage of the writing process. List in the space provided:

1. What type of choices should you be focusing on in the third and fourth draft?

_____

_____

_____

_____

2. What is your goal at this stage of the writing process?

_____

_____

3. How does editing a media script differ from the editorial process used in editing print copy? How is it similar? Enter your ideas in the space provided:

How is editing a media script similar to editing print copy?

_____

_____

_____

_____

_____

_____

_____

_____

In what ways does editing a media script differ from editing print copy?

_____

_____

_____

_____

_____

_____

_____

_____

MINI-LESSON: SCRIPT EDITING "DO'S & DON'TS"

The following suggestions may prove helpful to ensure the final polishing doesn't mar the overall effect of the shooting script.

DO'S:

• Do continue reading narration and/or dialogue aloud. Check for conversational quality and consistency of voice.

• Punctuate for the ear—not for the grammarians.

• Avoid awkward page breaks, especially relating to narration and dialogue. Make it easy on the talent.

• Maintain your sense of authorship and creative control. You are also one of the elite corps of readers. And you are the only one who can put various comments from other script readers into the narrative and visual style consistent with the total script.

• Maintain objectivity. Pressure to get the script into production often adds a sense of urgency that can lead to chaos. Keep a sense of humor. And remember: "scripts are never finished, they're merely abandoned."

DON'T:

• Let grammatical correctness interfere with conversational quality. Contractions, idioms and short declarative sentences are the hallmark of writing for the ear.

• Don't be fanatical about the visual descriptions. These are never read by your viewers. A shot description does not need to read like Shakespeare. If it conveys the essence of what you mean—don't belabor the point.

CHAPTER **9**

Sample Project Using Scriptwriting Worksheets

INTRODUCTION

This chapter contains a sample project—from initial assignment to revised and approved shooting script. It illustrates one writer's use of scriptwriting worksheets as well as appropriate writing products from each stage of the scriptwriting process.

The client for this project was the Dutchess County Tourism Promotion Agency in Hyde Park, New York. Karen Woods, the agency's Director, served as both client and subject matter expert. The production company was JonMari Communications; director James G. Libby; writer William Van Nostran.

I selected this project for illustration because everyone can relate to the non-technical subject matter. The program could be no more than 8 to 10 minutes in running time—so the writing samples and scripts are short and can be read quickly.

The project is also quite "real world." Because of budgetary and time constraints, much of the visual footage had to be culled from existing "stock" video footage and color slides provided by the many tourist and cultural attractions mentioned in the script. The challenge: find a way to incorporate visuals from diverse sources, integrating them into a stylistically cohesive video program.

Most of the writer's decisions at key points can be seen by reading the scriptwriting worksheets and resulting writing products. Occasionally, I've offered additional insights relating to the dynamics of this specific script development process—primarily as they affected various shooting script rewrites.

SCRIPTWRITING WORKSHEET 1
SELECTING THE MEDIUM FOR THE MESSAGE

WHAT TO DO: Answer the following questions as they relate to your specific project.

1. If you have no say in what medium you'll be writing for, enter that medium below:

    Video

    [If media selection is part of your assignment, skip ahead to question 4:]

2. Referring to the appropriate media chart on pages 16 through 23 of *The Scriptwriter's Handbook*, what specific strengths of this medium are likely to be most advantageous given what you know so far about the assignment?

    1. *Full motion when video footage is available.*

    2. *Video easily incorporates other media; i.e. slides; still photos, graphics, text etc.*

3. Referring to this same media chart, what specific weaknesses of this medium are likely to work against you given what you know so far about the assignment?

Video is often referred to as a "close-up" medium. Much of this subject matter, however, consists of massive exteriors, sweeping landscapes & vistas.

(Answer the next questions only if you are involved in media selection:)

4. If you have a say in what medium is selected for this project/assignment, return to this page to consider these questions after completing all the activities up to and including Chapter 4: Organizing Information.

    A. Given the nature of your content, what media seem best suited to deliver this message?

                                                 N.A.

    B. Explain why?

                                                 N.A.

    C. Given your audience, viewing environment and objectives, what media seem best suited to deliver this message?

                                                 N.A.

D. Explain why?

<u>N.A.</u>

5. Consider these additional factors:

A. How long a shelf-life is your project expected to have?

3 to 4 years

B. During this program's lifetime, is the information likely to change frequently?

_____ Yes   _X_ No

C. How will budget and/or production facilities/resources affect media selection?

<u>N.A.</u>

D. Does the due date affect media selection? If so, how?

No

6. Considering all factors, what is your medium of choice for this assignment?

<u>Video</u>

Why? Because it readily incorporates a variety of visual material from diverse sources and other media. It is also easily duplicated, shipped and viewed in cassette form.

7. If, for some reason, you are unable to write for your medium of choice, what medium would be the best alternative?

_____ N.A. _____

Why _____

_____

_____

8. After considering all these factors and discussing them with the client and producer as appropriate, what medium has been selected for your project?

Video

NEXT...

Answer questions 1 through 3 and return to the script development process. Or, if you've answered those questions already, move ahead to begin the script development process.

SCRIPTWRITING WORKSHEET 2: YOUR RESEARCH AGENDA

PROJECT: *Dutchess County Tourism Video*

Develop a List of Interview Contacts	What do you expect to learn from Interview?
Karen Woods	*Karen is both the subject matter expert and client who will distribute the completed program. As such, she'll have a major say in both what to include and how much emphasis various tourist attractions should receive. In addition, she'll provide objectives, audience profile and viewing situation.*
Tony Marks *Dutchess County Tour Bus Operator*	*By interviewing Tony, I can get the perspective of someone who books frequent area tours and knows what local attractions appeal to various demographic groups. Although "unofficial," such input will serve to either verify Karen's observations or provide added insights.*

Time Frame for Completion: *One Week*

Develop A List of Readings & Resource Materials

1. *Dutchess County Tourism Promotional Literature*

2. *Promotional literature from individual Dutchess County tourist attractions, cultural, recreational and other related points of interest, including seasonal events, restaurants and lodging.*

Time Frame for Completion: *Two Weeks*

Develop a List of Activities You'll Need to Do or See

Observation and first-hand experience is essential for this project. Several days should be allocated for visiting key tourist attractions, talking to tour guides and tourists, local merchants and developing an appreciation for the local color and characteristics of this segment of the historic Hudson Valley area.

Time Frame for Completion: Two Weeks

Will Questionnaires or Surveys Be Useful in Learning More About the Content, Organization or Audience?

<u>X</u> Yes _____ No

If "yes", describe the purpose of the Questionnaire or Survey?

Might be interesting to develop a questionnaire that could be used with tourists both before and after their Dutchess County visit.

Will you have the time and resources to conduct this research activity?

_____ Yes <u>X</u> No

Time Frame for Completion: _____

Other Research Activities
N.A.

Time Frame for Completion: _____

SCRIPTWRITING WORKSHEET 3: YOUR AUDIENCE PROFILE

WHAT TO DO: Write your initial understanding of the audience and the logistics of the "communication environment" in the space provided:

The primary target audience for this presentation ranges from about 45 years of age and older. This market segment is growing rapidly as baby boomers mature, become grandparents and, eventually, seniors.
Some characteristics of this group include:

- They are healthier and wealthier than previous generations their age. They are veteran business travelers.

- They're able to take advantage of mid-week travel bargains and often tour with grandchildren.

In addition, this market segment is frequently serviced by major tour operators who can use this video to encourage potential groups to include Dutchess County in their travel itinerary.

Assess the communication environment. Knowing what you do about the audience, the message and the dynamics of the viewing environment, is your viewing audience likely to be:

<u>X</u> Positive

____ Neutral

____ Negative

What factors lead you to this conclusion?

They will probably not be viewing the video if they do not have some initial interest in touring Dutchess County. At the very least, the target audience may be neutral.

After completing your research: Double-check your initial understanding of the audience and communication environment. Has it changed? If so, revise as necessary:

_____

_____

_____

_____

_____

_____

_____

SCRIPTWRITING WORKSHEET 4: YOUR PROGRAM OBJECTIVES

WHAT TO DO: Describe the overall, primary objective of your program in your own words:

Inform the audience of the tourist, cultural and natural attractions that make Dutchess County a good place to visit.

Inform the audience of the many restaurants, hotels/motels and other commercial establishments (antique shops, etc.) that cater to the visiting tourist.

Motivate the prospective visitor to actually make a tour to Dutchess County.

How would you categorize the primary objective? Check the appropriate type:

____ Informational

<u>X</u> Motivational

____ Instructional

In what ways, if any, will your program have to be motivational as well as informational or instructional?

This is a motivational program; but it has a large informational component. The more information about Dutchess County, the more diverse and rich the tourist possibilities, the more likely people will respond to the motivational message. Viewers should be motivated to take the next step toward planning a visit.

SCRIPTWRITING WORKSHEET 5: YOUR CRITICAL CONTENT

WHAT TO DO: To help identify the critical content of your program, answer the following questions. If you have difficulty completing this worksheet, you may not have sufficiently assimilated the content yet. Try to determine what areas you should research further.

1. List factors that tend to make your target audience receptive to the message.

    They will not be looking at the program unless they have an interest either in touring Dutchess County, specifically, or, at least, considering Dutchess County in making overall vacation plans. The wide variety and diversity of tourist attractions and cultural/recreational activities in Dutchess County offer something for almost any interest.

2. What factors, if any, might make the target audience respond negatively to the content or message?

    Many of the County's historical venues and antique shops will appeal more to older viewers. Ideally, the program will also show there are activities and attractions for younger people, families and children—especially at different seasons of the year. Also, since there is so much to tout about the County, there's the possibility of "information overload."

3. If you were a member of the viewing audience, what would you like to get out of this program?

    I'd want to see something there that would interest me in visiting. (In my case, that might be a cultural or arts-oriented activity or something of historical significance.)

    _____

    _____

    _____

4. How can you appeal to the self-interest of your audience to generate interest in the program?

    Illustrate diversity—Dutchess County has something for everyone.

    _____

    _____

    _____

5. Given your assessment of the objectives, the audience and the communication environment, what three to five content points are most critical? (Once you identify these topics, you must find ways to communicate these points effectively. Ideally, they become the big moments in the finished program.)

    1.   Dutchess County has something for everyone

    2.   There are both historical and cultural resources in the County

    3.   Dutchess County offers natural beauty. As part of the Hudson River Valley area, it affords tourists many recreational opportunities.

    4.   Dutchess County welcomes and accommodates tourists and visitors.

SCRIPTWRITING WORKSHEET 6: MATCHING FORMATS TO YOUR CONTENT

WHAT TO DO: Refer to your content outline. Select the key points of the presentation and enter each below. Then, for each key point, determine the Program Format you think will be most effective and enter in the space provided.

        In addition, identify a Program Format that could be used as an alternate method of presenting the same key point.

Key Point 1: Introduction to "Dutchess Past" & her county

            Most Effective Format: Visuals & Voice

            Alternate Format: Dramatization

Key Point 2: Hyde Park: Roosevelt Estate & Mrs. Roosevelt's Retreat (Val-kill)

            Most Effective Format: Visuals & Voice

            Alternate Format: Talking Head with Props

Key Point 3: Other historical mansions, museums & cultural attractions

            Most Effective Format: Visuals & Voice

            Alternate Format: Talking Head with Props

Key Point 4: Outdoor & recreational activities; including Rhinebeck Aerodrom

            Most Effective Format: Visuals & Voice

            Alternate Format: Talking Head with Props

Key Point 5: Culinary Institute & other dining places

            Most Effective Format: Visuals & Voice

            Alternate Format: Interviews

PART 2

WHAT TO DO: Now, answer the following questions by reviewing the selections you made for each key point.

1. Looking at the "Most Effective" formats, is there any danger your script will lack variety in format?

 __X__ Yes   ____ No

If you marked "Yes"...

Review the list of "Alternative Formats." Can you identify a logical solution?

 __X__ Yes

Describe your solution: Portray Dutchess County "Past" & Present" by on-camera live talent. Have Dutchess County Present interview various tourism site directors/proprietors. Budget precludes this option.

 __X__ No

Explain why the "Alternative Formats" fail to solve the problem you anticipate:

Since budget does not provide funds for on-camera talent and location shooting expenses, variety will have to come from use of off-camera narrative voice, pacing, transitional elements, music & special effects.

_____

_____

If you marked "No" for question 1, review the list of "Most Effective" Formats. Is there any danger of your script resulting in a "hodge-podge" of formats, with no single format dominating?

 ____ Yes

In this case, review the list of "Alternative Formats" to see if there is a solution to this problem.

Describe your solution:

_____

_____

 ____ No

In this case, explain why the formats you are combining will be compatible with one another:

_____

_____

SCRIPTWRITING WORKSHEET 7:
DETERMINING YOUR PROGRAM'S STRUCTURE

WHAT TO DO: Answer the following questions with your own scriptwriting project in mind.

1. Referring to your program objectives, audience analysis and critical content, which structural type best suits the needs of your program?

    ____ Advertised structure

    _X_ Unadvertised structure

    ____ A combination of the two

2A. (Answer if you intend to make the program structure apparent to the audience.) Why will **advertising** the structure work to your advantage in achieving the program's objectives?

    _____

    _____

    _____

    _____

    What visual or narrative cues and techniques could you employ to advertise the structure and provide reference points as the program unfolds?

    _____

    _____

    _____

    _____

2B. (Answer only if you choose to **conceal** the program structure from the audience.) Why will an **unadvertised** structure work to your advantage in achieving the program's objectives?

    We want the audience to be continually surprised by the variety of activities and attractions in Dutchess County.

    _____

    _____

    _____

    _____

What visual/narrative technique will you use to keep the audience "off-balance," unable to predict what will happen next?

1. Use of two distinct narrative voices

2. Free-flowing, associational type of content organization

_____

_____

_____

_____

_____

To keep the program from appearing random and haphazard, your script must still have an underlying structure or "spine" which the writer and director can follow. Describe the underlying structure of your program:

Use of two female narrators provides dual organizational perspectives: past and present.

3. Next, consider these questions about the chronological sequence of events that will unfold on screen.

   A. Think about the critical content that will become major scenes in your script. Use key words to describe these "big" scenes and list them below.

   Roosevelt Estate in Hyde Park

   Culinary Institute of America

   Rhinebeck Aerodrom

   Outdoor activities & nature

   Cultural Resources

   B. Can you think of a way to open the program that meets the requirements of a good opening scene or sequence of scenes? If so, describe below:

   Introduce and personify Dutchess County Past to provide audiences with a sense of historical perspective.

   If you're unsure about how to open the program—don't get stuck on the question. You can make this decision later.

C. What is your script building toward? What is the climax? The high point? Describe a closing scene or sequence that meets the requirements of a strong closing:

Dutchess County Past and Present come together to provide a sense of closure and completeness—a harmony between then and now.

SCRIPTWRITING WORKSHEET 8: DO YOU HAVE A STORY TO TELL?

WHAT TO DO: Referring to your own content, audience and objectives, brainstorm ways to humanize the message through storytelling techniques.

1. What kind of a story do I have to tell?

A story of personal experience and memory, as Dutchess County Past recalls the early days of the county and how it received its name.

2. Do you feel a need to humanize this message?

<u>X</u> Yes _____ No

If "yes," what are some ways to surprise your audience through vivid, meaningful storytelling techniques?

Employing a character narration to bring the Dutchess Maria Beatrice D'Este (Queen Mary) vividly to life.

If "no," justify your answer. In other words, why is this information so compelling that your target audience will be innately interested?

_____

_____

_____

_____

_____

_____

_____

_____

SCRIPTWRITING WORKSHEET 9: MAKING STYLISTIC DECISIONS

WHAT TO DO: Answer the following questions with your own project in mind.

1. Describe the overall tone or point-of-view you would like to take toward the subject matter:

    Dutchess County has two contrasting, distinctive personalities: the Past and the Present.

    _____

    _____

2. How will this attitude be communicated through visual cues?

    Use of two, contrasting picture frames to create a standard border:

    1. ornate & gilded = for scenes representing the Past

    2. simple & metallic = for action showing Dutchess County today

3. How will this attitude be communicated through narration, dialogue, music, sound, etc.?

    Use of two female narrators: Dutchess County Past and Dutchess County Present (They should have distinctive narrative styles, vocabulary and vocal qualities.)

    Use of contrasting musical styles from appropriate periods.

4. If you intend to mix contrasting styles (a comedic vignette within an otherwise serious piece), how will you ensure the two styles will function synergistically?

    _____

    _____.

    _____

    _____

    _____

    _____

    _____

    _____

SCRIPTWRITING WORKSHEET 10: DREAM A LITTLE

WHAT TO DO: Before getting practical—dream a little. Imagine if you had unlimited resources, time and talent to produce your own program. No limitations. No clients with negative attitudes. What would you do?

This is your time for the "daydreaming part." Describe the program you would like to write under ideal conditions with no limitations. It will be the most effective way to communicate the content to your target audience:

Ideally, we would use an actress to portray the Dutchess in period costume on camera. She would take us on a tour of the historical sites—addressing the camera. Then, at a specific transitional moment, we employ special effects to change the actress's costume, hairstyle and make-up—creating an on-camera transformation signifying the change to modern day Dutchess County. She would then continue as our personal tour guide.

SCRIPTWRITING WORKSHEET 11: APPLYING THE MATRIX TO YOUR CONCEPT

WHAT TO DO: You've considered your program's format, structure and style. Next, work at imagining the content in your head as a fully produced viewing experience. Try to "see" pictures that will appear on screen and "hear" narration, dialogue and sound.

Imagine the "chronological sequence of events" that will comprise the viewing or listening experience.

Evaluate your concept by answering the questions relating to the Concept Development Matrix.

1.   Briefly describe the concept in your own words:

The material is organized into two sections: historical attractions and sites versus present day activities. Past and Present are personified by Dutchess County Past and Present: two distinctive off-camera narrative voices.

2.   Now critically evaluate your concept by checking the appropriate item for each question.

    A.   Evaluate how well the concept functions as a "spine" to unify format, style and structure in terms of the program content.

        ____ Unsatisfactory

        ____ Marginal

        _X_ Satisfactory

        ____ Outstanding

B. Evaluate how appropriate the concept is for the target audience.

_____ Unsatisfactory

_____ Marginal

__X__ Satisfactory

_____ Outstanding

C. Evaluate how appropriate the concept is for the company or organization.

_____ Unsatisfactory

_____ Marginal

__X__ Satisfactory

_____ Outstanding

D. Evaluate the concept in terms of feasibility.

PRODUCTION TIME:

_____ Unsatisfactory

_____ Marginal

__X__ Satisfactory

_____ Outstanding

BUDGET & RESOURCES

_____ Unsatisfactory

_____ Marginal

__X__ Satisfactory

_____ Outstanding

E. Evaluate the concept's potential for synergistic visual and narrative expression.

_____ Unsatisfactory

_____ Marginal

_____ Satisfactory

__X__ Outstanding

F. Evaluate how well major program segments and formats will work together stylistically.

_____ Unsatisfactory

_____ Marginal

__X__ Satisfactory

_____ Outstanding

NOTE: A key moment will be the transition from Dutchess County Past to Dutchess County Present.

G. Evaluate how effectively the concept fulfills client expectations. Is it results-oriented, rooted in careful consideration of audience, viewing environment and objectives?

____ Unsatisfactory

____ Marginal

_X_ Satisfactory

____ Outstanding

3. Have you identified any significant flaws in your concept?

____ Yes   _X_ No

If "yes..."

• Either the strengths of the concept must outweigh potential liabilities, or...

• You must adjust the concept accordingly, or...

• You must go back to the "drawing-board" and develop a new concept.

SCRIPTWRITING WORKSHEET 12: ARE YOU READY TO WRITE A TREATMENT?

WHAT TO DO: Answering the following questions will tell you if you're prepared to write a treatment—a "sketch" of your vision of the ultimate viewing experience in chronological sequence.

1. Can you "see" and "hear" the program unfold as a chronological sequence of events in your mind?

_X_ Yes ____ No

If "No," go back over previous scriptwriting worksheets to see if you can stimulate mental sights and sounds.

Once you answer "yes," proceed to the remaining questions...

2. Describe how the program will open. Use words that describe "sights" and "sounds" the viewer will see and hear.

We hear a woman's voice, strong & authoritative as she introduces herself as the Dutchess. This is followed by MUSIC of the period. She begins to explain how twelve New York counties were established in 1683—and one was named for her. Then she invites the audience to come visit her County—Dutchess County, New York.

3. How does this opening "hook" the target audience? If you're uncertain, review the Audience Profile and Communication Environment descriptions.

By using the "sight & sound" capabilities of the video medium to bring a historical figure to life; personifying a physical location; extending an invitation to the viewing audience.

4. How does your opening answer the question: "What's in it for me?"

    By showing a variety of diverse people enjoying Dutchess County's many tourist offerings and attractions.

5. Write out your "vision" of the Body of the program. (It will probably take several pages, so use additional sheets of paper.) Use words that describe "sights" and "sounds". Focus on how the chronological sequence of events unfold on the screen. Don't get too detailed. Summarize key content.

    Dutchess County past describes Hyde Park, F.D.R.'s retreat, and Val-Kill, Mrs. Roosevelt's own "get away" while we view these historical sites which can be toured by present day visitors.

    Dutchess County Past also describes highlights of the Vanderbilt Estate and its restored Italian Gardens, as well as other spots of historical interest.

    Then, almost out of nowhere, the SOUND of an airplane engine pierces the air. This cues the transition for action footage of the Old Rhinebeck Aerodrom as Dutchess County Past says "to see some of the county's historical treasures—you have to look to the sky..." She explains the Rhinebeck Aerodrom as we feature the Museum buildings; then show antique aircraft in the sky. Suddenly, the sound of an antique aircraft engine changes to that of a modern sleek jet aircraft engine. This cues Narrator Two, who says something like: "There's more than history in Dutchess County..." then goes on to describe various contemporary attractions and family recreational opportunities.

6. Then, answer the following questions about the description of the program's body:

    A. Have you identified the primary visual images?

        __X__ Yes _____ No

    B. Have you identified the primary on and off-screen participants?

        __X__ Yes _____ No

    C. Have you described the primary locations and the action which occurs in them?

        __X__ Yes _____ No

    D. Have you described key transitions?

        __X__ Yes _____ No

    E. Have you described use of music, titles and supers, special effects, computer animation or other unusual techniques that effect production requirements?

        __X__ Yes _____ No

    F. Have you communicated a sense of the narrative and visual style?

        __X__ Yes _____ No

G. Did you communicate a sense of the "big" scenes and what will make them the most memorable moments of the program?

<u> X </u> Yes <u>＿＿</u> No

H. Could the client read your description and visualize how the program will unfold on the screen?

<u> X </u> Yes <u>＿＿</u> No

I. Could a producer or director use your treatment to address issues relating to production requirements, logistics, talent, editing and budgeting?

<u> X </u> Yes <u>＿＿</u> No

An answer of "No" to any of these questions may indicate your treatment is not fully developed. Go back and flesh out those areas that lack specifics.

7. Finally, describe how the program concludes. Again, use words that relate to the "sights" and "sounds" of the viewing or listening experience.

At the conclusion of the program, the voices of Dutchess County Past and Present will be heard interacting for the first time. As they issue a final invitation to tour the county, their "togetherness" symbolizes the duality of Dutchess County tourist attractions.

8. Does this conclusion provide a sense of completion?

<u> X </u> Yes <u>＿＿</u> No

9. Does the conclusion end on a high note—giving viewers more than a simple repetition of key points?

<u> X </u> Yes <u>＿＿</u> No

10. If action is required on the part of the audience, is it clear what they are supposed to do following the program?

<u> X </u> Yes <u>＿＿</u> No

11. Have you provided a "kicker"—something to leave your audience with a sense of satisfaction at the end?

<u> X </u> Yes <u>＿＿</u> No

An answer of "no" to any of these questions may signal your program simply "stops." Like a sales presentation, good media programs require a powerful closing.

Go back and work out a closing that drives your message home forcefully. It need not be long, but it must have a strong conclusion that is conveyed with impact!

SCRIPTWRITING WORKSHEET 13: VISUALS IN YOUR SCRIPT

WHAT TO DO: Before proceeding, answer the following questions about the visual material of your program:

1. Check the box which best describes the primary type of visual material you envision for your program:

    _X_ location action footage (Including some slides & photos)

    ____ studio setting

    ____ still photos or graphics

    ____ animated graphics

    ____ a combination
    Describe this mix:

    _____

    _____

    _____

    _____

2. Describe the primary function of your footage, visuals, graphics, photos and/or sets—i.e., Do they serve a specific purpose in communicating content; or, do they function more to set a mood or tone? You may, of course, use both type in your program.

    The primary function of visuals is to show the variety of tourist attractions available in Dutchess County. Capture the natural beauty and rustic charm of the region.

3. Describe the visual style or look you are aiming for in your program?

    My primary difficulty results from the diverse sources—mixing live action stock video footage with slides, etc. To ameliorate this problem, we will develop two stylized computer generated picture frames. One will appear in the highly ornate style of the Past; the second as a simple, elegant, modern frame. These frames will cue key transitions and integrate dissimilar visuals.

4. In a previous worksheet (Scriptwriting Worksheet 5, item 5), you identified the "big moments" of your program. These are the key points you want to be most memorable. Can you think of visually arresting, memorable images that correspond to these big moments? Describe below:

    Aerodrom footage, portrait of the Dutchess, scenic and tourist attractions.

5. What script page layout do you wish to use?

    _X_ Dual column video or slide format

    ____ Film script format

113

SCRIPTWRITING WORKSHEET 14: RESPONDING TO YOUR ROUGH DRAFT

WHAT TO DO: Give yourself the pleasure of being the first to read your draft script critically. Before revisiting your script, think about what you experienced getting a rough draft down on paper (or in the word processor). Decide what you'd like to focus on in responding to the draft by answering the following questions.

1. First, what are the strengths of your rough draft—those things you feel best about accomplishing up to this point?

   Concept is sound. Organization and structure works well. Even though the presentation is entirely "visuals and voice," it doesn't seem to be terribly predictable.

   _____

   _____

2. Without even reading your rough draft, list those elements of the script you believe still need improving or more attention:

   Style of the two character voices too similar. Needs greater contrast somehow.

   _____

   _____

Now—go ahead and read your draft script. Try to see again with fresh eyes...

3. Respond to what you have read. What do you consider the scripts strong points?

   Same as above.

   _____

   _____

4. What things do you want to fix?

   Certain segments too wordy. Still concerned about the narrative voice, style and contrast between Past & Present.

   _____

   _____

5. Can you make these adjustments on your own—or will you need direction/input from the client or content expert?

   <u> X </u> Yes _____ No

SCRIPTWRITING WORKSHEET 15: REVISION CHECKLIST

WHAT TO DO: Before submitting your first draft shooting script for review and discussion, make sure you've made your first draft as strong as possible. Use the following Revision Checklist as a guide.

1. ____ Have you read the script aloud and made changes accordingly?

2. ____ Have you read the script once focusing solely on content?

3. ____ Have you reviewed the draft in terms of the original objectives? Are you satisfied the draft achieves all objectives?

4. ____ Have you read the script once focusing on the sight and sound synergy?

5. ____ Have you read the script once focusing on your use of media production terminology?

6. ____ Have you reviewed the script focusing on pacing, the timing of various segments and overall length?

7. ____ Are you satisfied the script will result in an interesting viewing experience?

8. ____ Has the production task remained feasible given time and budgetary parameters?

9. ____ Has the draft shooting script remained faithful to the original treatment? If it differs, are you satisfied the new approach represents an improvement? Can you justify the new direction?

10. ____ Is there anything about the shooting script that might need clarifying in a covering memo or in introductory remarks at the script review session? If so, plan how to handle this subject.

SCRIPTWRITING WORKSHEET 16: ANALYZING FEEDBACK

WHAT TO DO: Every project brings unique revision requirements. Once you return from the initial review session, assess what needs to be accomplished in your rewrite. Use the following sheet to determine the extent and nature of revisions on your own project.

Content Related Revisions:

____ Content errors need correcting

____ Important content is missing

____ Too much script time devoted to specific content points

____ Content needs restructuring

____ Content not sufficiently visualized

Narrative Related Revisions:

____ Narration too "talky". Omit needless words.

____ Narrative voice (or voices) convey inappropriate sense of tone.

____ Narrative voice inconsistent in style and tone.

Visualization Related Revisions:

____ Content insufficiently visualized

____ Inappropriate visuals at times

____ Execution of visuals, graphics or sets go beyond what is feasible given budget or time parameters.

____ Client, content expert, producer or director having difficulty "picturing" graphics or settings from verbal description. (Often, a good solution is to storyboard a segment or do set design renderings.)

Conceptual Problems:

____ Script deviates significantly from treatment. (May be positive or negative.)

____ Client or others uncomfortable with concept now that it is fully developed.

____ Shooting script falls short in reaching the promise of the original concept as conveyed in treatment.

____ Other. Describe below

_____

_____

_____

_____

_____

_____

_____

CHAPTER 10

Sample Project:

Dutchess County Tourism Brochure

NOTE TO WRITING SAMPLES: CREATIVE STRATEGY & TREATMENT

For this particular project, I prefaced the Treatment itself with a short explanation of the Creative Strategy, feeling a complete understanding of the rationale for the strategy being employed would put the Treatment in context, making it easier to envision.

Remember—the Treatment describes the chronological sequence of events. Do not clutter treatments with discussions of other issues.

PROJECT: **DUTCHESS COUNTY TOURISM VIDEO BROCHURE**
SHOOTING PROPOSAL
REVISED DRAFT: OCTOBER 12, 1990

CREATIVE STRATEGY

"If everything is important—then nothing is important..."

As you yourself recognize, the difficulty in developing a brief (7 to 8 minute) video brochure on Dutchess County is that there is so much to include.

Unlike a print presentation, however, where readers can selectively focus on specific attractions that interest them, a film cannot be all-inclusive.

In the same way that a motion picture has "major stars" backed by a supporting cast, the Dutchess County videobrochure needs to have certain "starring" attractions—supported by glimpses of other attractions treated as "cameo appearances."

With this in mind—there is a natural structural division between historical and contemporary attractions.

Therefore, I recommend two female narrators—one who takes the role of The Dutchess Past; the second playing The Dutchess Present. This in itself

PROJECT: **DUTCHESS COUNTY TOURISM VIDEO BROCHURE**
SHOOTING PROPOSAL
REVISED DRAFT: OCTOBER 12, 1990

provides a structural way of organizing the material. And the change of voice, offering two distinct perspectives on the overall content, provides change of pace and contrast.

At the same time--the content must highlight certain featured attractions--with supporting attractions being mentioned visually or verbally through music montages strategically placed throughout the piece. Viewers can then be referred to collateral print materials where they can find details onwhatever attractions have the greatest appeal to them.

This story-telling device is perhaps best illustrated by reading the following Treatment. . .

TREATMENT

We Fade UP on...

A woman's voice—it has the character of age, but is still strong and authoritative (a la Coleen Dewhurst).

"I am the Dutchess Maria Beatrice D'Este. You probably know me better as—Queen Mary of England..."

The MUSIC at this moment is of the period--perhaps a few woodwinds. The shots focus on the lushness of the countryside and outdoors at different times of the year.

"In 1683, twelve New York counties were established by the British Crown. This verdant valley by the Hudson was named for me--Dutchess County. A lot has happened here since 1683... so I invite you to come and see the jewels in my crown for yourself. Come visit--Dutchess County, New York..."

MUSIC now hits full--it is more up tempo. A fuller, orchestral sound. We do a matching MONTAGE with shots which now feature people--people enjoying themselves in a variety of activities.

As this montage ends, we feature the scroll which unfurls with the program title: "The Dutchess Invites You!"

We touch BLACK, then UP on shots of the Roosevelt Hyde Park Library and Museum. The voice of "Dutchess Past" offers a brief description and

PROJECT: **DUTCHESS COUNTY TOURISM VIDEO BROCHURE**
SHOOTING SCRIPT
REVISED DRAFT: OCTOBER 29, 1990

invitation--highlighting that the museum of the venerable Roosevelt
family manor on the banks of the Hudson contains a vast number of arti-
facts representative of F.D.R.'s political and personal life--including
his collection of ship models and memorabilia from days as Secretary of
the Navy.

The Dutchess also invites us to Val-Kill--describing how this became Mrs.
Roosevelt's personal cottage for use by her and her friends. "Today, visitors can walk the same trails the former First Lady walked so often..."
She highlights that individual and group tours of both F.D.R.'s Museum
and Val-Kill go on throughout the year...

..."for a look at the way of life of wealthy Hudson Valley landowners at
the turn of the century, The Vanderbilt Mansion is a splendid representa-
tion of the gilded age..." We feature a few highlights of the Vanderbilt
Estate and restored Italian Gardens...

We will have Dutchess Past mention a few additional sites of historical
interest as well as antique shops and the many Bed & Breakfast opportunities..

...then, almost out of nowhere, the SOUND of an airplane engine pierces
the air... this SOUND EFFX cues a transition to the action footage of the
Old Rhinebeck Aerodrome. "Not all the museums and historical sights of
Dutchess County are on the ground," explains Dutchess Past. "Visitors to
the Rhinebeck Aerodrome are witness to a museum in the sky!"

We feature a few facts about the Aerodrome weekend air shows, showing Museum Buildings full of old aeroplanes, engines and cars--highlighting
that "this is a great place to bring youngsters--and don't forget cameras
and video camcorders..."

As we follow a plane in the air--the SOUND EFX changes to a more
modern engine and the antique plane DISSOLVES into a small, sleek pas-
senger plane of present day vintage. This CUES our major transition to
the voice of...

...the Dutchess Present. (In contrast to our first Narrator, the Dutchess
Present has a more youthful, yet equally engaging vocal quality.)
"There's more than history in Dutchess County," she says. "Today's
Dutchess County is vibrant and alive with activities of all kind..."

The MUSIC, which is now a more contemporary, upbeat jazz style theme,

PROJECT: **DUTCHESS COUNTY TOURISM VIDEO BROCHURE**
SHOOTING PROPOSAL
REVISED DRAFT: OCTOBER 12, 1990

comes up full for a brief MONTAGE of various activities. The Dutchess Present begins by highlighting the wide variety of outdoor recreational pleasure available through state and local parks. Here is where we might briefly provide seasonal highlights--hiking in the spring; boating and fishing on the Hudson in the summer; "pick your own" apples harvesting in Autumn; cross-country skiing and ice skating in the winter...

...and, whereas Dutchess Past highlighted inns and Bed & Breakfasts, Dutchess Present speaks about some of the more modern accommodations and restaurants. She also features the Culinary Institute of America--where America's "master chefs of tomorrow learn their craft today." We discover that anyone can enjoy one of the 4,000 meals prepared here daily and served in four public restaurants. "Here, one can enjoy true gourmet dining at prices that won't starve your pocketbook."

This leads us into the fact that Dutchess County is also part of New York state's wine country. "Many vineyards dot the rolling hills. Tours and tasting go on year round."

Dutchess Present also highlights cultural activities in the area--including art galleries, theatre, symphony orchestra, etc.

The climax of the film brings the voices of Dutchess Past and Dutchess Present together at the same time. They offer a "spoken duet" which summarizes and encapsulates the richness of their historical, bountiful and diverse county. As the film concludes, viewers are referred to the Dutchess County Tourism Promotion Agency for further information and details on seasonal activities.

Dutchess Present concludes with a final invitation: "Come join us soon to make your own Dutchess County history and memories today!"

FADE TO BLACK...

NOTES TO SCRIPT EXCERPTS AND REVISIONS

This project demonstrates familiar problems encountered in revision—in this case relating primarily to voice. Since the creative strategy was designed to contrast Dutchess County Past and Present through two different off-camera female narrators—a distinctive "voice" and speech pattern for each would do much to enhance the contrast.

Following are two samples of dialogue from the *first draft* of the original shooting script—the first two pages of the script, featuring Dutchess County Past . . . and the first paragraphs of narration from Dutchess County Present . . .

PROJECT: **DUTCHESS COUNTY TOURISM VIDEO BROCHURE**
SHOOTING SCRIPT
REVISED DRAFT: OCTOBER 29, 1990

VIDEO	AUDIO
FADE UP ON:	MUSIC: (A theme and arrangement of the period--perhaps a few woodwinds and drums.)
An opening MONTAGE that may take one of several forms. If possible, we begin with period photos and artwork--including a portrait of the Dutchess herself.	DUTCHESS PAST: (Her voice has the character of age, but is still strong and authoritative--a la Coleen Dewhurst). I AM THE DUTCHESS MARIA BEATRICE D'ESTE. YOU PROBABLY KNOW ME BETTER AS--QUEEN MARY OF ENGLAND...
We develop a SPECIAL GRAPHIC--an ornate style frame to create a border around these shots.	
The shots focus on the lushness of the coyntryside and outdoors at different times of the year.	IN 1683, THE BRITISH CROWN ESTABLISHED TWELVE NEW YORK COUNTIES. THIS VERDANT VALLEY ON THE MAJESTIC HUDSON RIVER WAS NAMED IN MY HONOR--DUTCHESS COUNTY.
The final shot in this sequence is a STILL FRAME of the Dutchess' hands. ACTION begins as she unfurls a scroll--	MUCH HAS TRANSPIRED IN THIS BUCOLIC SETTING SINCE THE YEAR 1683... SO I ENTREAT YOU-- COME EXPERIENCE THE BOUNTY OF MY COUNTY FOR YOURSELF. YOUR PRESENCE IS REQUESTED IN DUTCHESS COUNTY--AT YOUR EARLIEST CONVENIENCE!
SUPER:	
In ornate calligraphy: "I invite you... ...to Visit... Dutchess County Past"	MUSIC: (Hits full--it is more up to tempo. A fuller, orchestral sound.)

PROJECT: **DUTCHESS COUNTY TOURISM VIDEO BROCHURE**
SHOOTING SCRIPT
REVISED DRAFT: OCTOBER 29, 1990

VIDEO	**AUDIO**
We touch BLACK, then UP on STILL FRAMES of the Roosevelt Hyde Park Library and Museum...	<u>DUTCHESS PAST</u>: YOUR THREE-TERM PRESIDENT, FRANKLIN D. ROOSEVELT, ONCE SAID: "WHEN A MAN HAS BEEN AWAY A LONG TIME, IT IS SOMETIMES NECESSARY FOR HIM TO GET TO A PLACE WHERE HE CAN SEE THE FOREST AS WELL AS THE TREES."
...on CUE, the ORNATE FRAME ZOOMS forward and off-screen as the MONTAGE goes to FULL ACTION.	
MONTAGE of b&w historical photos INTERCUT with video footage.	FOR MR. ROOSEVELT, THAT PLACE WAS THE VENERABLE ROOSEVELT FAMILY MANOR OVERLOOKING THE HUDSON IN HYDE PARK.
	MR. ROOSEVELT, THE FIRST PRESIDENT TO ARRANGE FOR HIS PRESIDENTIAL PAPERS TO BECOME NATIONAL PROPERTY, DONATED THE HISTORIC FAMILY HOME AS LIBRARY AND MUSEUM. OPENED TO THE PUBLIC SINCE 1941--VISITORS ARE WELCOME STILL--ANY DAY EXCEPT FOR MAJOR HOLIDAYS.
	'TIS NOT ALL BOOKS AND PAPERS. YOU'LL SEE MR. ROOSEVELT'S OWN MOTOR CARRIAGE, EQUIPPED WITH SPECIAL HAND CONTROLS SO HE COULD TOUR DUTCHESS COUNTY ROADS. OR VIEW HIS FINE NAUTICAL COLLECTION OF MODEL SHIPS--MANY CRAFTED BY HIS OWN HANDS.

123

PROJECT: **DUTCHESS COUNTY TOURISM VIDEO BROCHURE**
SHOOTING SCRIPT
REVISED DRAFT: OCTOBER 29, 1990

VIDEO:	**AUDIO:**
...ON CUE, THE MODERN FRAME ZOOMS forward and off-screen as the shot goes into FULL ACTION...	<u>DUTCHESS COUNTY PRESENT</u>: THERE'S MUCH MORE TO EXPERIENCE IN <u>TODAY'S</u> DUTCHESS COUNTY THAN HISTORY. FOR THOSE WHO LIKE OUTDOOR AC-TIVITIES, TODAY'S DUTCHESS COUNTY HOLDS SOMETHING IN STORE EVERY SEASON...
...initiating a MONTAGE of contemporary Dutchess County attractions.	
We see golf courses, and the wide range of outdoor recreational pleasures available through state and local parks.	IN SPRINGTIME, HIKE ALONG NATURE TRAILS IN ONE OF OUR STATE PARKS AND FORESTS...
Here is where we provide seasonal highlights--hiking in the spring; boating and fishing on the Hudson in the summer...	...IN SUMMER, FISH, SWIM OR ENJOY A HUDSON RIVER BOAT TOUR...
... "pick your own" apple harvesting in Autumn; crosscountry skiing and ice skating in the winter...	...OR PLAY ONE OF OUR SEVEN CHAMPIONSHIP GOLF COURSES.
	... "PICK YOUR OWN" APPLE ORCHARDS AND PUMP-KIN PATCHES DELIGHT FALL VISITORS...
	...OUR WINTER SNOWS ARE PERFECT FOR SLEDING, CROSS-COUNTRY SKIING AND ICE SKATING.
FREEZE FRAME on screen of winery...	DUTCHESS COUNTY'S ALSO NEW YORK STATE WINE COUNTRY. YOU CAN TOUR SEVERAL AREA VINE-YARDS...
... on CUE, the MODERN FRAME ZOOMS forward and off-screen as vineyard shots go to FULL ACTION...	

NOTES TO SCRIPT EXCERPTS AND REVISIONS (cont'd)

As originally drafted, there is not much in the style of the narrative voices themselves to set the two characters apart.

In responding to this first draft, the director, Jim Libby, suggested a more distinct contrast could be achieved if Dutchess County Past spoke in the style of old English. Some of the director's suggested changes are indicated on the following pages . . .

PROJECT: **DUTCHESS COUNTY TOURISM VIDEO BROCHURE**
SHOOTING SCRIPT
REVISED DRAFT: OCTOBER 29, 1990

VIDEO	AUDIO
FADE UP ON:	MUSIC: (A theme and arrangement of the period--perhaps a few woodwinds and drums.)
An opening MONTAGE that may take one of several forms. If possible, we begin with period photos and artwork--including a portrait of the Dutchess herself.	DUTCHESS PAST: (Her voice has the character of age, but is still strong and authoritative--a la Coleen Dewhurst). ~~I AM THE~~ MY NAME IS
We develop a SPECIAL GRAPHIC--an ornate style frame to create a border around these shots.	DUTCHESS MARIA BEATRICE D'ESTE. ~~YOU PROBABLY KNOW ME~~ I WAS BETTER ⌐KNOWN AS--QUEEN MARY OF ENGLAND... (WIFE OF WILLIAM, THE ___.)
The shots focus on the lushness of the coyntryside and outdoors at different times of the year.	THE YEAR OF IN 1683, THE BRITISH CROWN ~~ESTABLISHED~~ DESIGNATED TWELVE NEW YORK COUNTIES. THIS VERDANT VAL-
The final shot in this sequence is a STILL FRAME of the Dutchess' hands. ACTION begins as she unfurls a scroll--	LEY ON THE MAJESTIC HUDSON RIVER WAS ~~NAMED~~ GIVEN THE NAME ~~IN MY HONOR~~--DUTCHESS COUNTY, IN MY HONOR.
BETTER OLDE ENGLISH WORDS?	MUCH HAS TRANSPIRED IN THIS BUCOLIC SETTING SINCE THE YEAR 1683... ~~SO~~ ⌐HENCE I ENTREAT YOU-- NAMESAKE COME EXPERIENCE THE BOUNTY OF MY ~~COUNTY~~ FOR THYSELF ~~YOURSELF~~. YOUR ~~PRESENCE~~ AUDIENCE IS REQUESTED IN ⌐ANON! DUTCHESS COUNTY--~~AT YOUR EARLIEST CONVE-~~ ~~NIENCE!~~
SUPER:	
In ornate calligraphy:	MUSIC: (Hits full--it is more up to tempo. A fuller, orchestral sound.)
"I invite you... ...to Visit... Dutchess County Past"	" YOUR PRESENCE IS FORMALLY REQUESTED IN THE COUNTY OF DUTCHESS, STATE OF NEW YORK "

126

PROJECT: **DUTCHESS COUNTY TOURISM VIDEO BROCHURE**
SHOOTING SCRIPT
REVISED DRAFT: OCTOBER 29, 1990

VIDEO	AUDIO
We touch BLACK, then UP on STILL FRAMES of the Roosevelt Hyde Park Library and Museum...	*[handwritten: ┌─INTREPID]* DUTCHESS PAST: YOUR THREE-TERM PRESIDENT, FRANKLIN D. ROOSEVELT, ONCE SAID: "WHEN A MAN HAS BEEN AWAY A LONG TIME, IT IS SOMETIMES NECESSARY FOR HIM TO GET TO A PLACE WHERE HE CAN SEE THE FOREST AS WELL AS THE TREES."
...on CUE, the ORNATE FRAME ZOOMS forward and off-screen as the MONTAGE goes to FULL ACTION.	
MONTAGE of b&w historical photos INTERCUT with video footage.	FOR MR. ROOSEVELT, THAT PLACE WAS THE VENERABLE ~~ROOSEVELT~~ FAMILY MANOR OVERLOOKING THE HUDSON IN HYDE PARK.

[handwritten note: BETTER OLDE ENGLISH WORDING]

MR. ROOSEVELT, THE FIRST PRESIDENT TO ARRANGE FOR HIS PRESIDENTIAL PAPERS TO BECOME NATIONAL PROPERTY, DONATED THE HISTORIC FAMILY HOME AS LIBRARY AND MUSEUM. OPENED TO THE PUBLIC SINCE 1941--VISITORS ARE WELCOME STILL--ANY DAY EXCEPT FOR MAJOR HOLIDAYS.

'TIS NOT ALL BOOKS AND PAPERS. YOU'LL SEE MR. ROOSEVELT'S OWN MOTOR CARRIAGE, EQUIPPED WITH SPECIAL HAND CONTROLS SO HE COULD TOUR *[handwritten: MY MAJESTIC]* ~~DUTCHESS~~ COUNTY ROADS. OR VIEW HIS FINE NAUTICAL COLLECTION OF MODEL SHIPS--MANY CRAFTED BY HIS OWN HANDS.

NOTES TO SCRIPT EXCERPTS AND REVISIONS

The author integrated many of these changes into the second draft shooting script. The client, Karen Woods of the Dutchess County Tourism Promotion Agency, was not totally comfortable with this approach. Her concern: that the voice of the Dutchess might sound too aristocratic; taking on a patronizing, condescending tone toward the target audience.

As a writer, I was caught between two equally valid, yet totally *contradictory*, responses to a draft script. Viewed purely from the standpoint of developing a distinctive narrative voice—Mr. Libby's direction had validity. But the client knows the audience best. And when Ms. Woods expressed concerns—highlighting specific words such as "bucolic", "anon", "intreprid" and "venerable"—an equally valid viewpoint had to be considered.

Scripts are never written in a vacuum. And the presence of conflicting directions in feedback, although often frustrating, is not unusual. This is because those who respond to draft scripts read the material from differing perspectives and identify specific concerns based on their point of view.

In this case, the client appreciated the writer's dilemma. A compromise version was hammered out—one that attempted to retain some old English flavor while judiciously avoiding the potential for "snobbishness" or "snootiness" in tone. Here is the writer's next version:

PROJECT: **DUTCHESS COUNTY TOURISM VIDEO BROCHURE**
APPROVED SHOOTING SCRIPT
NOVEMBER 7, 1990

VIDEO:	**AUDIO:**
FADE UP ON:	<u>MUSIC</u>:(A theme and arrangement of the period--perhaps a few woodwinds and strings. Telemann chamber music or 17th century recorders.)
An opening MONTAGE that may take one of several forms. If possible, we begin with period photos and artwork--including an attractive portrait of the Dutchess herself.	<u>DUTCHESS PAST</u>: (Her voice has the character of age, but is still strong and authorita-tive--a la Coleen Dewhurst). MY NAME IS DUTCHESS MARIA BEATRICE D'ESTE. I WAS BETTER KNOWN AS--QUEEN MARY OF ENGLAND...
We develop a SPECIAL GRAPHIC--an ornate style frame to create a border around these shots.	
The shots focus on the lushness of the contry-side and outdoors at dif-ferent times of the year.	IN THE YEAR 1683, THE BRITISH CROWN DESIG-NATED TWELVE COUNTIES IN NEW YORK. THIS VER-DANT VALLEY ON THE MAJESTIC HUDSON RIVER WAS GIVEN THE NAME--<u>DUTCHESS</u> COUNTY, A MOST GRA-CIOUS HONOR FOR ME.
The final shot in this sequence is a STILL FRAME which changes to a parch-ment looking document in the frame.	MUCH HAS TRANSPIRED IN THIS SETTING OF GREAT NATURAL BEAUTY SINCE THE YEAR 1683... HENCE I ENTREAT YOU--COME EXPERIENCE OUR TREASURES
On cue, handsome old Eng-lish script appears on the parchment... <u>SUPER</u>:	FOR YOURSELF. YOUR PRESENCE IS REQUESTED IN DUTCHESS COUNTY--AT YOUR EARLIEST CONVE-NIENCE!
In ornate calligraphy:	
Your Presence Is Formally requested in the County of Dutchess, State of New York	<u>MUSIC</u>: A fuller, orchestral sound. More of a Vivaldi flute concerto sound.)

PROJECT: **DUTCHESS COUNTY TOURISM VIDEO BROCHURE**
APPROVED SHOOTING SCRIPT
NOVEMBER 7, 1990

VIDEO:	AUDIO:
We touch BLACK, then UP on STILL FRAMES of the Roosevelt Hyde Park Library and Museum...	DUTCHESS PAST: YOUR FAMOUS THREE-TERM PRESIDENT, FRANKLIN D. ROOSEVELT, ONCE SAID: "WHEN A MAN HAS BEEN AWAY A LONG TIME, IT IS SOMETIMES NECESSARY FOR HIM TO GET TO A PLACE WHERE HE CAN SEE THE FOREST AS WELL AS THE TREES."
...on CUE, the ORNATE FRAME ZOOMS forward and off-screen as the MONTAGE goes to FULL ACTION.	FOR MR. ROOSEVELT, THAT "PLACE" WAS THIS STATELY FAMILY MANOR OVERLOOKING THE HUDSON RIVER IN HYDE PARK.
MONTAGE of b&w historical photos INTERCUT with video footage.	MR. ROOSEVELT WAS THE FIRST PRESIDENT TO MAKE HIS PRESIDENTIAL PAPERS NATIONAL PROPERTY. HE DONATED THE HISTORIC FAMILY RESIDENCE AS LIBRARY AND MUSEUM. 'TIS NOT ALL BOOKS AND PAPERS, THOUGH. YOU'LL SEE MR. ROOSEVELT'S OWN MOTOR CARRIAGE, SPLENDID MODEL SHIP COLLECTION AND OTHER FAMILY MOMENTOS.
	OPENED TO THE PUBLIC IN 1941--YOU ARE WELCOME STILL--EVERY DAY EXCEPT FOR MAJOR HOLIDAYS.
A FINAL shot is of Val-Kill...	VAL KILL, MRS. ROOSEVELT'S RETREAT, WAS BUILT IN THE 1920s. A SHORT DISTANCE FROM
...on CUE, the ORNATE FRAME ZOOMS forward and off-screen as the MONTAGE goes to FULL ACTION.	THE ROOSEVELT HOME, YOU MAY MEANDER THE SAME FOOT PATHS THE FIRST LADY

NOTES TO SCRIPT EXCERPTS AND REVISIONS (cont'd)

As always, execution effects the final impression on the viewing audience as well as the writing itself. In this instance, the client took time to attend the voice-over recording session to provide immediate feedback and approve final takes.

The complete shooting script, in its final draft follows:

PROJECT: **DUTCHESS COUNTY TOURISM VIDEO BROCHURE**
APPROVED SHOOTING SCRIPT
NOVEMBER 7, 1990

VIDEO:	**AUDIO:**

FADE UP ON:

An opening MONTAGE that may take one of several forms. If possible, we begin with period photos and artwork--including an attractive portrait of the Dutchess herself.

MUSIC:(A theme and arrangement of the period-- perhaps a few woodwinds and strings. Telemann chamber music or 17th century recorders.)

We develop a SPECIAL GRAPHIC--an ornate style frame to create a border around these shots.

DUTCHESS PAST: (Her voice has the character of age, but is still strong and authorita- tive--a la Coleen Dewhurst). MY NAME IS DUTCHESS MARIA BEATRICE D'ESTE. I WAS BETTER KNOWN AS--QUEEN MARY OF ENGLAND...

The shots focus on the lushness of the contry- side and outdoors at dif- ferent times of the year.

IN THE YEAR 1683, THE BRITISH CROWN DESIG- NATED TWELVE COUNTIES IN NEW YORK. THIS VER- DANT VALLEY ON THE MAJESTIC HUDSON RIVER WAS GIVEN THE NAME--DUTCHESS COUNTY, A MOST GRA- CIOUS HONOR FOR ME.

The final shot in this sequence is a STILL FRAME which changes to a parch- ment looking document in the frame.

MUCH HAS TRANSPIRED IN THIS SETTING OF GREAT NATURAL BEAUTY SINCE THE YEAR 1683... HENCE I ENTREAT YOU--COME EXPERIENCE OUR TREASURES FOR YOURSELF. YOUR PRESENCE IS REQUESTED IN DUTCHESS COUNTY--AT YOUR EARLIEST CONVE- NIENCE!

On cue, handsome old Eng- lish script appears on the parchment...
SUPER:

In ornate calligraphy:

Your Presence Is Formally requested in the County of Dutchess, State of New York

MUSIC: A fuller, orchestral sound. More of a Vivaldi flute concerto sound.)

PROJECT: **DUTCHESS COUNTY TOURISM VIDEO BROCHURE**
APPROVED SHOOTING SCRIPT
NOVEMBER 7, 1990

VIDEO:	**AUDIO:**
We touch BLACK, then UP on STILL FRAMES of the Roosevelt Hyde Park Library and Museum...	DUTCHESS PAST: YOUR FAMOUS THREE-TERM PRESIDENT, FRANKLIN D. ROOSEVELT, ONCE SAID: "WHEN A MAN HAS BEEN AWAY A LONG TIME, IT IS SOMETIMES NECESSARY FOR HIM TO GET TO A PLACE WHERE HE CAN SEE THE FOREST AS WELL AS THE TREES."
...on CUE, the ORNATE FRAME ZOOMS forward and off-screen as the MONTAGE goes to FULL ACTION.	
	FOR MR. ROOSEVELT, THAT "PLACE" WAS THIS STATELY FAMILY MANOR OVERLOOKING THE HUDSON RIVER IN HYDE PARK.
MONTAGE of b&w historical photos INTERCUT with video footage.	
	MR. ROOSEVELT WAS THE FIRST PRESIDENT TO MAKE HIS PRESIDENTIAL PAPERS NATIONAL PROPERTY. HE DONATED THE HISTORIC FAMILY RESIDENCE AS LIBRARY AND MUSEUM. 'TIS NOT ALL BOOKS AND PAPERS, THOUGH. YOU'LL SEE MR. ROOSEVELT'S OWN MOTOR CARRIAGE, SPLENDID MODEL SHIP COLLECTION AND OTHER FAMILY MOMENTOS.
	OPENED TO THE PUBLIC IN 1941--YOU ARE WELCOME STILL--EVERY DAY EXCEPT FOR MAJOR HOLIDAYS.
A FINAL shot is of Val-Kill...	VAL KILL, MRS. ROOSEVELT'S RETREAT, WAS BUILT IN THE 1920s. A SHORT DISTANCE FROM THE ROOSEVELT HOME, YOU MAY MEANDER THE
...on CUE, the ORNATE FRAME ZOOMS forward and off-screen as the MONTAGE goes to FULL ACTION.	

133

PROJECT: **DUTCHESS COUNTY TOURISM VIDEO BROCHURE**
APPROVED SHOOTING SCRIPT
NOVEMBER 7, 1990

VIDEO: **AUDIO:**

                                              SAME FOOT PATHS THE FIRST LADY TROD TO ESCAPE

                                              THE PRESS OF PUBLIC LIFE.

A sequence of shots show-
ing several historic   BUT DUTCHESS COUNTY HISTORY GOES SO MUCH FUR-
buildings. They appear in
the ornate gold frame and   THER BACK THAN THE ROOSEVELT ERA. IN MOST
FLIP electronically from
one to another.   EVERY VILLAGE, HISTORIC COLONIAL AND REVOLU-

                                TIONARY WAR HOMES, CHURCHES AND ARTIFACTS

                                BECKON.

                                THE VAN WYCK HOMESTEAD, ORIGINALLY BUILT FOR

                                THE CONTINENTAL ARMY, IS SAID TO BE THE SET-

                                TING OF JAMES FENIMORE COOPER'S NOVEL, <u>THE</u>

                                <u>SPY</u>.

SHOTS of Clinton House   THE CLINTON HOUSE IN POUGHKEEPSIE HOUSES PER-
and museum collection.
                                MANENT AND ROTATING EXHIBITS OF THE DUTCHESS

                                COUNTY HISTORICAL SOCIETY...

Shots of Young-Morse His-   ... AND IF YOUR INTEREST RUNS TO THE SCIEN-
toric Site.
                                TIFIC--VISIT THE YOUNG-MORSE SITE, HOME OF

                                SAMUEL MORSE HIMSELF. THE ORIGINAL MORSE

                                TELEGRAPH IS ONE OF MANY ITEMS ON EXHIBIT.

As we follow antique air-   <u>SOUND EFFEX</u>: (Almost out of nowhere, the SOUND
planes in flight...
                                of an airplane engine pierces the air...)

134

PROJECT: **DUTCHESS COUNTY TOURISM VIDEO BROCHURE**
APPROVED SHOOTING SCRIPT
NOVEMBER 7, 1990

VIDEO:	**AUDIO:**
MONTAGE of shots showing air show and museum buildings full of old aeroplanes, engines and cars.	<u>DUTCHESS PAST</u>: YET NOT ALL DUTCHESS COUNTY MUSEUMS ARE EARTHBOUND. TURN YOUR EYES TO THE HEAVENS AT THE OLD RHINEBECK AERODROME AND WITNESS THRILLING ANTIQUE AIR SHOWS!
	<u>MUSIC</u>: (World War I military band theme.)
	<u>DUTCHESS PAST</u>: RE-LIVE THE ERA OF THE RED BARON AT HUMOROUS AND INFORMATIVE DAREDEVIL AIR SHOWS HELD WEEKENDS FROM MAY TO OCTOBER...
	<u>ACTUALITY AUDIO</u>: (Sound Effx of planes and air show announcer's narrative.)
	<u>DUTCHESS PAST</u>: 'TIS A WONDEROUS SITE TO BEHOLD, SO BRING THE CHILDREN AND BY ALL MEANS, RECORD YOUR ADVENTURES ON FILM AND VIDEOTAPE.
We TRANSITION to STILL FRAMES from the Mills Estate, bordered again by the gilded, ornate frame.	<u>MUSIC</u>: (Transitional theme--something in the mode of rag-time music.)
	<u>DUTCHESS PAST</u>: FOR A LOOK AT WEALTHY HUDSON VALLEY LANDOWNERS' TURN-OF-THE-CENTURY LIVING, THE ELEGANT MILLS MANSION IS A SPLENDID

PROJECT: **DUTCHESS COUNTY TOURISM VIDEO BROCHURE**
APPROVED SHOOTING SCRIPT
NOVEMBER 7, 1990

VIDEO:	**AUDIO:**
...on CUE, the ORNATE FRAME ZOOMS forward and off-screen as the MONTAGE goes to FULL ACTION.	EXAMPLE OF WHAT YOUR AUTHOR, MARK TWAIN, DUBBED: "THE GILDED AGE..."
We feature a few high-lights of the Mills Mansion, Montgomery Place and ending on Vanderbilt Estate and restored Italian Gardens.	MONTGOMERY PLACE, INCLUDES A "PICK-YOUR-OWN" APPLE ORCHARD.
	BUT THE MOST OPULENT GILDED AGE MANOR IS THE VANDERBILT MANSION NATIONAL HISTORIC SITE.
	IN SUMMER, A RESTORED ITALIAN GARDEN BLOSSOMS WITH OVER ONE-THOUSAND ROSE BUSHES AND MORE THAN FOUR THOUSAND PERENNIALS...
DISSOLVE TO:	OTHER GARDEN ATTRACTIONS IN THE COUNTY INCLUDE INNISFREE GARDEN...
Other Garden attractions.	
	...AND THE MARY FLAGLER CAREY ARBORETUM FEATURING NATURE TRAILS AND PICNIC AREAS.
	OF COURSE, NOT ALL DUTCHESS COUNTY HISTORIC BUILDINGS ARE MUSEUMS. IF THE SUN SETS ON YOUR FUN AND YOU'VE TIME TO LINGER...

PROJECT: **DUTCHESS COUNTY TOURISM VIDEO BROCHURE**
APPROVED SHOOTING SCRIPT
NOVEMBER 7, 1990

VIDEO:	**AUDIO:**
MONTAGE of shots featuring Inns framed with ORNATE border...	...ENJOY A STAY IN ONE OF MY COUNTY'S MANY TRADITIONAL, COMFORTABLE BED AND BREAKFAST INNS...
Shots of antiquing appear in ornate border.	PURCHASE FINE HEIRLOOMS FROM A WIDE SELECTION OF DUTCHESS COUNTY ANTIQUE DEALERS...
A shot of Beekman Arms in ornate border...	... OR STAY AT THE NATION'S OLDEST LANDMARK INN.
SPECIAL ELECTRONIC EFFX as it flips as though on a center pole...	MUSIC: (Historical style theme segues to...
...to REVEAL...	MUSIC: (Modern, contemporary jazz style theme.)
... a shot from contemporary lodging. The picture frame goes from gilded gold...	DUTCHESS PRESENT: (In contrast to our first Narrator, Dutchess Present has a more youthful, yet equally engaging vocal quality.)
... to modern, brushed chrome gold or silver look.	...OR, IF YOU PREFER...
SUPER: **In modern typeface:** **You are Cordially Invited to Visit... Dutchess County Present**	...LET US PAMPER YOU IN ONE OF OUR LUXURIOUS, MAJOR HOTELS FEATURING ALL THE MODERN CONVENIENCES.

PROJECT: **DUTCHESS COUNTY TOURISM VIDEO BROCHURE**
APPROVED SHOOTING SCRIPT
NOVEMBER 7, 1990

VIDEO:	**AUDIO:**
... on CUE, the MODERN FRAME ZOOMS forward and off-screen as the shot goes to FULL ACTION...	EXPERIENCE THE OTHER SIDE OF DUTCHESS COUNTY-- A VERY VIBRANT, MODERN PLACE TO VISIT. AND FOR THOSE WHO LIKE OUTDOOR ACTIVITIES, TODAY'S DUTCHESS COUNTY HOLDS SOMETHING IN STORE EVERY SEASON...
... initiating a MONTAGE of contemporary Dutchess County attractions.	
We see golf courses, and the wide range of outdoor recreational pleasures available through state and local parks.	IN SPRINGTIME, HIKE ALONG NATURE TRAILS IN ONE OF OUR STATE PARKS AND FORESTS...
Here is where we provide seasonal highlights--hiking in the spring; boating and fishing on the Hudson in the summer...	... IN SUMMER, FISH, SWIM OR ENJOY A VARIETY OF WATER SPORTS...
	... OR PLAY ONE OF OUR EIGHT PUBLIC GOLF COURSES LOCATED THROUGHOUT THE COUNTY.
... "pick your own" apple harvesting in Autumn; crosscountry skiing and ice skating in the winter...	... "PICK YOUR OWN" APPLE ORCHARDS AND PUMPKIN PATCHES DELIGHT FALL VISITORS...
	... WHILE OUR WINTER SNOWS ARE PERFECT FOR SLEDING, CROSS-COUNTRY SKIING AND ICE SKATING.
FREEZE FRAME on scene of winery...	
... on CUE, the MODERN FRAME ZOOMS forward and off-screen as vineyard shots go to FULL ACTION...	DUTCHESS COUNTY'S ALSO WINE COUNTRY. YOU CAN TOUR SEVERAL AREA VINEYARDS...

PROJECT: **DUTCHESS COUNTY TOURISM VIDEO BROCHURE**
APPROVED SHOOTING SCRIPT
NOVEMBER 7, 1990

VIDEO:	**AUDIO:**
Shots of Vineyard activities...	... WHERE TOASTS AND TASTINGS ARE TRADITIONAL. AND WHEN IT COMES TO TASTING...
FREEZE FRAME on scene of CIA...	
... on CUE, the MODERN FRAME ZOOMS forward and off-screen as the shot goes to FULL ACTION...	YOU CAN SAMPLE THE WORK OF TOMORROW'S GREAT CHEFS AT HYDE PARK'S WORLD-RENOWNED CULINARY INSTITUTE OF AMERICA.
... MONTAGE featuring kitchen activities followed by elegant tableside presentation.	AS A VISITOR TO AMERICA'S OLDEST CULINARY SCHOOL, YOU CAN ENJOY ONE OF THE MANY DIFFERENT CUISINES PREPARED DAILY AND SERVED IN FOUR ELEGANT DINING ROOMS OPEN TO THE PUBLIC. EXPERIENCE TRUE GOURMET DINING--AT MODERATE PRICES.
Continue MONTAGE with footage depicting modern dining...	BUT FINE DINING IS NOT LIMITED TO THE CULINARY INSTITUTE...
	... YOU CAN CAP OFF A DUTCHESS COUNTY DAY WITH CUISINES TO PLEASE EVERY PALATE.
MAP appears in picture frame. At first it highlights location of county relative to NYC and Albany...	YOU'LL FIND ALL THESE ATTRACTIONS EASY TO REACH. CENTRALLY LOCATED BETWEEN NEW YORK CITY AND ALBANY, DUTCHESS COUNTY'S ACCESSIBLE BY CAR, RAIL, AIR AND BUS.

PROJECT: **DUTCHESS COUNTY TOURISM VIDEO BROCHURE**
APPROVED SHOOTING SCRIPT
NOVEMBER 7, 1990

VIDEO:	**AUDIO:**
... then ZOOMS forward to fill frame. SPECIAL EFX as we <u>SUPER</u> driving tour routes.	WHEN DRIVING, EXPLORE THE COUNTY'S 800 SQUARE MILES BY USING ONE OF OUR SELF-DRIVING TOUR BROCHURES AS A GUIDE.
FREEZE FRAME on symphony orchestra with chrome picture frame border...	<u>MUSIC</u>: (Symphony orchestra piece up full. Something Romantic or a bit contemporary.)
... the MUSIC plays for a few moments... ... then the shot goes to FULL ACTION as MODERN FRAME ZOOMS forward and off-screen.	<u>DUTCHESS PRESENT</u>: IF THE ARTS ARE YOUR PAS-SION--MANY TREASURES AWAIT YOU IN PRESENT DAY DUTCHESS COUNTY...
MONTAGE of cultural activities available in the area...	... YOU'LL FIND SOMETHING FOR EVERY TASTE...
	... THEATRE...
	... THE HUDSON VALLEY SYMPHONY ORCHESTRA...
	... AND ARTS AND CRAFTS RANGING FROM THE TRADITIONAL...
	... TO THE VERY CONTEMPORARY.
FEATURE Vassar College exterior...	VISITORS WITH A PENCHANT FOR ART MUST TOUR THE VASSAR COLLEGE ART GALLERY. WHEN MATTHEW VASSAR PLANNED HIS COLLEGE IN THE 1860's...

PROJECT: **DUTCHESS COUNTY TOURISM VIDEO BROCHURE**
APPROVED SHOOTING SCRIPT
NOVEMBER 7, 1990

VIDEO:	**AUDIO:**
Continue MONTAGE with artwork from Vassar collection.	... HE MADE IT THE FIRST IN AMERICA TO IN-CLUDE A MUSEUM ART COLLECTION. THE COLLECTION RANGES FROM THE CLASSICS...
Feature classics...	
DISSOLVE to modern paintings.	... TO CONTEMPORARY MASTERS--INCLUDING THE HUDSON RIVER SCHOOL OF LANDSCAPE PAINTERS.
FINAL MONTAGE...	DUTCHESS COUNTY PAST: SO WHETHER ONE IS A SERIOUS STUDENT OF HISTORY...
	DUTCHESS COUNTY PRESENT: ... OR LOOKING FOR SCENIC BEAUTY OR A SPECIAL EVENT...
	DUTCHESS PAST: ... WE OFFER A DIVERSE MIX OF THE PAST...
	DUTCHESS PRESENT: ... AND THE PULSATING PRESENT. SO, IF YOU'RE COMING WITH A TOUR GROUP...
	DUTCHESS PAST: ... PLANNING A FAMILY OUTING...
	DUTCHESS PRESENT: ... OR SEEK A WEEKEND RE-TREAT FOR TWO...

PROJECT: **DUTCHESS COUNTY TOURISM VIDEO BROCHURE**
APPROVED SHOOTING SCRIPT
NOVEMBER 7, 1990

VIDEO:	**AUDIO:**

DUTCHESS PAST: ... RICH, BOUNTIFUL DUTCHESS
COUNTY AWAITS THE PLEASURE OF YOUR COMPANY.

SUPER: MUSIC: (Theme UP FULL to end.)

Final titles and credits.

As the film concludes,
viewers are referred to
the Dutchess County
Tourism Promotion Agency
for further information
and details on seasonal
activities.

FADE TO BLACK

Introduction to Leader's Guide and Answer Key

This section reviews suggested answers to various General Activities. It is designed for two potential users:

Instructors: If you are using *The Scriptwriter's Workbook* in a classroom setting, the "To Instructors" notes offer ideas on how to use specific activities to generate student involvement and discussion in class.

Individual Writers: If you are using the workbook on your own, simply complete activities in sequence. At the end of each chapter, you may wish to review the suggested answers and material titled: "To Instructor & Individual Student."

Remember—these are suggested answers based on experience using activities with students in workshops and courses. But there is always room for additional points and alternative perspectives.

Leaders's Guide and Answer Key

CHAPTER 1: MEDIA: A MESSAGE

General Activity 1.1: Thinking about Media Scriptwriting (on page 5)

To the Instructor: Use this activity to introduce basic concepts about the functions of a media script and the scriptwriter's role. Give students a few minutes to develop their own list working with a neighbor or in buzz groups.

Then, conduct a class discussion.

Ask for answers in each column.

Write typical answers on a flip chart. You'll find answers similar to those below.

To Instructor & Individual Student: In many ways, scriptwriting is no different than any other type of writing. Steps in the writing process, in particular, are rather universal.

On the other hand, scriptwriting is a unique genre. Scripts are written in the language of media production terminology. It requires unusually strong visualization skills coupled with an ability to write narrative copy that is easily spoken.

Ironically, few people *read* the writer's finished script. Rather, it is used as a set of instructions on how to make a specific viewing or listening or interactive experience aimed at a target audience.

The last item is something of a trick question. Almost any answer is partly correct. Clearly, media writing, especially when using dramatization, is much like playwriting; even more like screenplay writing. (But that is not a *literary* genre.) Like the poet, media writers must paint strong visual images and use great economy of language. Like the novelist, the media writer must be able to tackle difficult, sometimes abstract subjects. Often, the media writer needs the brevity of the short story writer.

In a sense—it brings us full circle to the notion that, in many ways, writing media scripts is no different than writing for other genres.

General Activity 1.1: Thinking about Media Scriptwriting (on page 5)

Ways in which scriptwriting for media is no different from other genres:	Ways in which scriptwriting for media differs from other writing genres:
• Requires research • Requires understanding of assignment • Author needs to know audience • Requires conceptual skills • Involves decisions regarding style, structure, storytelling technique, etc. • Involves creating a first draft • Use of imaginative skills • May employ dialogue, description and other narrative techniques.	• Requires visualization • Is written in production terminology • Audience will see and hear; not read • Uses music, sound effects and special effects • Must be spoken as narration or dialogue • Tends to be collaborative in nature • Time constraints usually important consideration • Must be feasible to produce given resources, time and budget

What other literary forms or genres is media writing most similar to and why?

Playwriting, Screenwriting, Poetry, Non-Fiction Writing, Cartooning, etc.

Review Activity

To Instructor & Individual Student: Review activities cover material presented in specific chapters or sections of *The Scriptwriter's Handbook* text. They are one way of testing your understanding of the material presented in the chapter. Feel free to refer to the text when necessary.

In classroom situations, discussion of review questions and answers is a good way to prepare for more in-depth class activities.

This review activity covers material presented in Chapter 2 of *The Scriptwriters Handbook*.

1. Put a "P" by those media which create and display visual images photographically, an "E" by those that create and display visuals electronically, and "NA" by those which do not apply:

    NA or P Print

    NA Audio Cassette

    E Videotape

    P Multi-Image Slide Presentations

    P Film

    E PC-Based Multi-Media

2. Put an "M" by all those media which are full-motion media:

    _____ Print

    _____ Audio Cassette

    M Videotape

    _____ Multi-Image Slide Presentations

    M Film

    M PC-Based Multi-Media (given proper hardware/software combinations)

3. The illusion of motion results from a phenomenon known as: *persistence of vision*

4. Identify the full motion medium associated with the following frames per second. Place "NA" by any that do not apply.

    24 frames per second *Film*

    26 frames per second N.A.

    30 frames per second *Video*

    32 frames per second N.A.

5. Place a "1" by those media having the best image resolution:

  _____ Video

  _1_ Film

  _1_ 35mm slides

  _____ PC-based multi-media

6. Place a check-mark by those media which provide immediate recording and playback capability:

  _X_ Video

  _____Film

  _____Multi-Media Slide Presentation

  _X_ Audio Cassette

  _____PC-Based Multi-Media

  _____Print

7. Place a check-mark by those media which generally require some type of computer programming or special authoring to create and playback the finished product:

  _X_ Multi-Image Slide Presentation

  _____ Film

  _X_ PC-Based Multi-Media

  _____ Audio Cassette

  _____ Video Teleconference

  _X_ Videowall Presentation

8. Place a check-mark by those media which are ideally suited for viewing by a large audience of 100 people or more:

  _X_ Film

  _____ Print

  _X_ Multi-Image Slide Presentation

  _____ Audio Cassette

  _____ PC-Based Multi-Media

  _____ Video

9. Place a check-mark by those media which are ideally suited for a one-on-one sales presentation in the customer's office:

_____ Film

__X__ Print

_____ Multi-Image Slide Presentation

__X__ Audio Cassette

__X__ PC-Based Multi-Media

__X__ Video

10. What is a "hybrid" medium? Give at least one example.

Two or more media which come together to form a new media experience by interacting with one another.

Example: The CD-ROM combines a mixture of video, audio, graphics, text and animation with the interactivity of computer software to create a new media experience.

11. Why is it necessary for a writer to know the characteristics, strengths and weaknesses of various media?

Media writers should be skilled in scripting for all media; capable of combining sight and sound experiences using appropriate technologies to maximize the strengths of the chosen medium. Versatility comes from familiarity with each medium and how they may interact.

CHAPTER 2: THE SCRIPTWRITING PROCESS

General Activity 2.1: The Writing Process (on page 13)

To the Instructor: Have the class complete the activity, working alone or with a neighbor. Give them about 5 to 7 minutes.

Then, conduct a class discussion.

Ask for answers in each column.

Write typical answers on a flip chart. You should build a list similar to that at the right.

To Instructor & Individual Student: Surprisingly, many writers do not have a good understanding of the writing process. Much of what writers do is problem solving; making decisions. It's important to work within an overall framework so you know where you are in the process at any given time. You want to ask yourself the right questions at the right *time*.

Writing is never an exact science. Organizing the task into a step-by-step process keeps you from being overwhelmed by the assignment. Moving methodically forward through the writing process also builds confidence in the emerging work.

Although the overall writing process is similar for almost all types of writing, scriptwriting makes special demands. You'll learn how to adapt the overall writing process to the specific needs of the scriptwriter.

At this point, take a closer look at the overall writing process you will use throughout the course of developing your own script.

General Activity 2.1: The Writing Process (on page 13)

What do you do first, second, third, etc.? Jot down the steps you take in the space below. You could also do this in collaboration with a classroom partner.

Step 1: *Get The Assignment*

Step 2: *Find out about audience & objectives*

Step 3: *Research, gather material, observe, interview*

Step 4: *Develop Content Outline*

Step 5: *Develop Creative Approach*

Step 6: *Write treatment*

Step 7: *Get client & SME feedback; director & producer input*

Step 8: *Write first draft*

Additional Steps:

Get additional client & SME feedback

Revise and polish accordingly

Review Activity 2 (on pages 14 and 15)

To Instructor & Individual Student: This review activity covers material presented in the Introduction to Part I of *The Scriptwriter's Handbook* text. Answering these questions and class discussion, where possible, provides an overview of the entire scriptwriting process prior to going into detailed study of each step in the process. Feel free to refer to the text when necessary.

WHAT TO DO: The following is a list of writing products which conclude each major stage of the scriptwriting process. Fill in the blank by describing the stage of the media writing process they are associated with. Then answer the questions that follow:

Content Outline	*Assimilation*
Media Treatment	*Rehearsal*
Audience Profile	*Assimilation*
Revised Shooting Script	*Revision*
Objectives	*Assimilation*
First Draft Shooting Script	*Drafting*
Completed Shooting Script	*Editing*

1. At what stage of the scriptwriting process would it be appropriate to hear this comment from the client:

   "I don't like this approach at all. It's too serious a subject to be treated with humor."

   Stage in process: Rehearsal

   Why? Justify your answer.

   Creative concepts should be presented to the client in treatment form at the rehearsal stage to make sure the client approves the concept before investing the time in writing a complete shooting script.

   At what stage would it be inappropriate to hear such a comment? Drafting

   Why? Justify your answer.

   The client should not be surprised by the creative concept, nor asked to approve your creative concept this late in the process.

2. An in-house producer tells you:

   "I've been concerned about this approach all along. But now that I see it fully scripted, I have to say—I don't think it's appropriate for our organization."

   Stage in the process: Drafting

   Is this an appropriate stage in the process to hear this response? Possibly

   Why? Justify your answer.

   It sounds as though the client may have given the writer the benefit of the doubt; approving a concept with reservation. It probably would have been more helpful to the writer to communicate concerns at the treatment stage. Perhaps they could have been resolved successfully at that time.

General Activity 2.2: Functions of the Media Script (on page 16)

To the Instructor: Have the class complete the activity, working alone or with a neighbor. Give them about 5 to 7 minutes.

Then, conduct a class discussion.

Ask for answers.

Write typical answers on a flip chart. You should build a list similar to that at the right.

To Instructor & Individual Student: Scripts serve a variety of functions at various points throughout the production planning and execution process. All the functions listed at the right (and others which are not listed) are legitimate functions of a shooting script.

It's important to realize that media production is generally a collaborative process—the work of many skilled crafts people. The writer is the only one who performs his or her job without a script. All other members of a crew or production team are working from the script.

Ironically, once the media program is completed, the script becomes obsolete. And so, the script is, in a very real sense, a document used to create something else, much like an architect's plans.

Functions of a media script include:

- Serves as a blueprint for production
- Indicates content
- Indicates program flow and structure
- Cues specific events
- Coordinates pictures and sound
- Provides instructions on how to make program in writer's head
- Provides tool for budgeting and production planning
- Communicates message to intended audience
- Meets client needs

General Activity 2.3: Identify Script Readers (on page 16)

To the Instructor: Have the class complete the activity, working alone or with a neighbor. Give them about 5 to 7 minutes.

Then, conduct a class discussion.

Ask for answers in each column.

Write typical answers on a flip chart. You should build a list similar to that below. It helps to use a similar order as well.

To Instructor & Individual Student: In an earlier activity, it was pointed out that the script is meant to be read by only a few. The writer communicates to the audience in the form of a "listening" or "viewing" experience.

Unfortunately, several important readers of your scripts will not be skilled at visualizing the viewing experience on paper. Often, clients and subject matter experts focus only on narration and dialogue—erroneously thinking that is where all content resides. In a well-written, fully realized media script, however, visualization and visual style are equally important.

Later, we'll look at techniques for helping clients and content experts visualize: use of treatments, renderings and storyboards, script page layouts and the psychology of presenting scripts to your client.

Identify SCRIPT READERS by TITLE:	*This READER will focus on:*	
Client	Content/Effectiveness	skilled/**unskilled**
Producer	Content, cost, production needs	**skilled**/unskilled
Content Experts	Content	skilled/**unskilled**
Director	Production needs, logistics, cost, style	**skilled**/unskilled
Boss	Effectiveness	**skilled/unskilled**
Production Team	Each reads from own perspective	**skilled**/unskilled
Legal/Executives	Problems, avoiding risk	skilled/**unskilled**

*May vary, depending on the boss' media experience.

CHAPTER 3: COLLECTING INFORMATION FOR THE SCRIPT
General Activity 3.1: What Makes the Difference? (on page 19)

To the Instructor: This class discussion activity is a good way to introduce the Assimilation Stage. Give students four to five minutes to complete each column—drawing on one positive and one unsuccessful writing experience.

Then, conduct a class discussion.

Ask various students to describe their project and what factors made it successful or unsuccessful.

Write typical answers on a flip chart. After several students have shared experiences, a pattern of responses usually emerges—similar to those below.

To Instructor & Individual Student: "Without caring there is no real writing." Writers succeed in an assignment when they feel the subject is important; understand the material; have insight into the audience and can identify personally with the outcome of their writing.

To achieve this close identification with content and audience, writers also need support. In media writing that support takes the form of:

• Clients capable of articulating their needs

• Helpful subject matter experts

• Access to research sources and material and people

• A measure of creative control (opportunity for personal expression)

• Appropriate budgets, production resources and time lines

The goal of research, therefore, is to assimilate the content; make it a part of yourself so you identify personally with the subject matter and goals of the project. Assimilation also means you understand the subject well enough to bring your own insights to bear on the project.

When such personal interest or commitment is lacking—inferior, mediocre writing invariably results.

Think of a time you were personally "invested" in a piece of writing. It may be a letter, a poem, a report, a corporate memo. Jot down reasons *why* you connected with this piece of writing.	Think of a time you did not "connect" with a piece of writing. As a result, the writing was difficult, drudgery. Jot down reasons why you found this writing a chore.
Writing Experience:	Writing Experience:
Reasons:	Reasons
• Understood subject • Understood purpose for writing • Believed in project • Cared about outcome • Understood audience • Had creative control • Had good support; access to resources • Had a strong, appropriate creative strategy	• Did not know subject • Lacked cooperation & support • Lacked creative control • Served too many masters; wrote for committee • No interest in subject • Felt overwhelmed by task • Lacked belief in project • Had conflicting direction • Could not come up with good creative strategy

Now, answer this question: What made the difference?

Good writing results from strong, personal commitment to project by all involved. Writer must feel empowered and in control. "Without caring, there is no real writing."

Review Activity

To Instructor & Individual Student: This review activity, covering material presented in Chapter 3 of *The Scriptwriters Handbook*, should help clarify the distinction between the act of research and the process of assimilation. Feel free to refer to the text when necessary.

Research is the period during which the scriptwriter *assimilates* content. To paraphrase Howard Gardner, by assimilating the collected information we are able to think about a topic in an original way. The material must be so organized in your mind that you readily juxtapose and combine it in a variety of unexpected, flexible ways.

When you assimilate content, it mixes with other accumulated knowledge. This is how writers develop metaphors, analogies and other ways of communicating content in a clear, concise, interesting manner.

Don't get ahead of yourself at this stage of the writing process and start thinking about *how* to use media to present the information. The creative concept comes later in the Rehearsal Phase.

1. What are the three main goals of research?

   To determine what the media presentation will be about...

   To collect & assimilate content...

   To determine the communication environment...

2. What is the "core question?"

   What do you want to say, to whom, for what purpose?

3. How does the "core question" relate to the three main goals of research?

   "What do you want to say" yields information about content "to whom" yields insight into the audience and viewing environment "for what purpose" yields information about objectives

4. There are many ways to conduct research. Brainstorm various methods the inquiring scriptwriter can use to gather useful information about the topic or assignment.

Read about it	*Talk to people about it*
Experience it; Do It; Perform Tasks	*Watch other media presentations*
See it in action	*Visit a location*

5. What is the difference between "research" and "assimilation?"

   Research is the act of collecting content. By assimilating content, the writer makes it part of his/her being and is able to think originally about the material.

6. What are some signs that you have collected sufficient information to proceed to the next step of the scriptwriting process?

You begin hearing same answers time & again...

You correctly anticipate answers to questions...

You exhaust your supply of subjects & questions...

You complete all tasks on your research agenda...

7. Why is the assimilation process important to the writer?

By making the subject yours, you are able to write with authority, confidence and enthusiasm, unlocking the key to personal creativity.

CHAPTER 4: ORGANIZING INFORMATION
Review Activity

To Instructor & Individual Student: This review activity covers material presented in Chapter 4 of *The Scriptwriters Handbook*. It should result in a clear understanding of the writer's first three writing products for presentation to the client and subject matter expert. These writing products provide the insight the writer needs to determine what content is crucial to communicating the message based on the client's expectations for the program.
  Feel free to refer to the text when necessary.

1. Your Action Plan begins with three important writing products:

  • Audience Profile

  • Objectives

  • Content Outline

  What is the overall purpose of these three documents?

  They communicate findings and results of your research to the client, producer and subject matter experts.

2. How does the audience's pre-disposition toward the subject matter of the communication influence the scriptwriter's task?

  An apathetic or skeptical audience will need to have their interest aroused or be convinced of the credibility of the information being communicated. Often, gaining interest or establishing credibility is as important to the communication's success as the content itself.

3. How does the viewing situation influence the scriptwriter's task?

  The dynamics of viewing in a large group, small group, or, individually, as well as the setting (home vs. trade show) and whether an audience is captive, all influence decisions regarding style, format, and program structure as well as the overall creative concept.

4. What are four types of media program objectives and how do they differ?

Type of Objective	*Characteristics*
Informational	Does not ask audience to act on information presented
Motivational	Persuades viewer to change attitude
Behavioral	Instructs audience on how to change behavior
Entertainment	Engages audience emotionally; makes for enjoyable viewing experience

5. How does a content outline for a media script differ from content outlines for more traditional types of print writing assignments?

There is no difference

General Activity 4.1: Identifying Program Objectives (on page 30)

To the Instructor: This short exercise will verify that students are distinguishing between informational, motivational and instructional or behavioral objectives. Have students complete the activity on their own.

Then, conduct a class discussion.

Ask for responses. Discuss the possible answers. Most are relatively clear cut although some program examples may involve more than one objective.

To Instructor & Individual Student: It's vital to distinguish between these three types of program objectives. Since objectives represent client expectations, you should become adept at formulating and stating objectives. When programs involve more than one type of objective, you also need to identify which type of objective is the driving force behind the program.

WHAT TO DO: Read through the list of program subjects. Although not phrased as specific objectives, most can be fairly typically classified as a media project with either an informational, motivational or behavioral objective. Write the type of objective you think each program best exemplifies in the space provided. Is the program primarily informational, instructional or motivational in nature?

1. A videotape on what constitutes sexual harassment: More than likely, this is an informational program. To the extent that the program discourages sexual harassment in the workplace, it could also be motivational.

2. A corporate television news program: Informational

3. A short multi-image module on leadership to kick-off a management conference:

Motivational

155

4. A videotape introducing company benefits to new employees:

Informational. To the extent that the program encourages employees to make informed choices, it could also be motivational. If the program covers how to sign up for benefits, it is also instructional.

5. An audio cassette providing general background on epilepsy for individuals who have just been diagnosed as having epilepsy:

Informational

6. A multi-media computer program on how to use advanced, high-end accounting software:

Instructional

7. Is there a role for entertainment in corporate or instructional media program design?

<u>X</u> Yes   _____ No

8. Justify your response in the space provided:

Programs succeed to the extent that they engage the audience's mind and heart. Entertainment plays a large role in developing programming that is original, surprising and innovative. Predictability is generally what leads to boredom and disinterest.

Another element of entertainment, humor and comedy, is sometimes ideally suited to driving home points in memorable ways. Just because a subject is serious doesn't mean we need to be solemn in writing about it.

General Activity 4.2: Focusing on Critical Content (on page 32)

To the Instructor: This activity helps novice writers understand that they cannot identify the critical content in any assignment without a thorough understanding of audience, viewing environment, objectives and the strengths and weaknesses of the medium for which they are writing. Have students complete the activity on their own or working with a neighbor.

Then, conduct a class discussion.

Ask for responses. Discuss the possible answers.

To Instructor & Individual Student: As writing coach Donald Murray points out: "Most people think writers write with words. We don't. We write with information." Writers always accumulate more information than they can possibly use in the finished script.

As such, critical content focusing is the process of filtering the information at your disposal so you include only the most vital information in your script. Critical content is never an absolute—it is always relative depending on the needs of the audience, the viewing environment, the objectives and the strengths and weaknesses of various media.

Determining critical content is a filtering process. You evaluate information to decide what to include in the script and what to discard. This activity gets you thinking about the selection criteria you use in this process of sifting and winnowing information.

WHAT TO DO: List criteria you can use to evaluate the information you've collected during research to determine the critical content points.

Program objectives.

The audience's knowledge of and attitude toward the message and topic.

What the audience needs to know at the end of the program.

The viewing environment.

What content is best suited to communicating via the medium you're writing for and what other media may be part of the overall communication experience.

CHAPTER 5: IDEA DEVELOPMENT

General Activity 5:1 The Scriptwriter's Choices (on page 36)

To the Instructor: This activity helps beginning writers realize that writing is problem solving and decision-making. Have the class brainstorm answers either in small buzz groups or working with a neighbor.
   Then, conduct a class discussion.
   Ask for answers, writing key words or phrases on a flip chart or board. Go for quantity. Almost any factor the scriptwriter must consider qualifies.
   Then introduce the role of the Rehearsal phase in giving the scriptwriter the time to consider these issues, to experiment and ultimately make some major writing choices about the creative direction his or her script will take.

To Instructor & Individual Student: Up to this point, the creative possibilities for your script are unlimited. During the rehearsal phase, however, you'll make important decisions about the concept you wish to employ that will set you down a specific creative path.
   Make such choices consciously so you will be confident explaining the rationale for your decisions in the context of the audience, objectives, content and media you have chosen. Certain practical production realities also influence your choices at this stage. Budget, production resources, availability of talent, graphic possibilities and the deadline must eventually be factored into your decisions.
   That doesn't mean you should always "play it safe," never taking risks. But know why you are willing to take the risk and the benefits that will accrue in meeting program objectives.

WHAT TO DO: Consider some of the many choices media scriptwriters must make—not choices regarding the content of the program, but choices relating to the creative treatment of the material as a viewing experience.
   Brainstorm a list of the kinds of choices media writers must make before beginning to draft a script.

What the chronological sequence of events will be. How to open, close and order the flow of information. What visuals will help tell the story. Style—documentary, presentational, serious, humorous, etc. Whether to have an on or off-camera narrator. Whether interviews can help tell the story or create credibility. The role of music and sound effects. Use of special effects, graphics and animation. Whether dramatization can help convey content. Pacing and use of change and contrast to gain attention and hold audience interest.

Review Activity: Idea Development (on page 36)

To Instructor & Individual Student: This review activity covers material presented in Chapter 5 of *The Scriptwriter's Handbook* text. It provides a way of testing your understanding of the function of the Rehearsal phase of the scriptwriting process. Feel free to refer to the text when necessary.

In classroom situations, discussion of review questions and answers is a good way to prepare for more in-depth class activities.

WHAT TO DO: Answer the following questions. Feel free to refer back to the Idea Development chapter when necessary.

1. Professional writer and teacher of writing Donald Murray made an important discovery when he allowed a colleague to study his writing methodology. Fill in the blanks. If you don't recall the exact percentages, take a guess—then return to the Idea Development chapter to see how close you were to the actual findings.

   Amount of writing time Murray spent collecting information & planning:

   Three-fifths

   Amount of time Murray actually spent writing:

   Two-fifths

   What is the significance of this finding to all writers?

   Often, we try to begin drafting prematurely. A better product usually results when more time is spent identifying and solving problems in the Assimilation and Rehearsal stages.

2. William Goldman is quoted discussing the importance of structure in writing screenplays. Structure is equally important to the media writer. What three decisions does the scriptwriter make when determining the proper structure for a script:

   A. What material to *include.*

   B. What material to *exclude.*

   C. The *placement* of that material from *beginning* to *end.*

3. List several different points of view a writer can take in expressing the identical content:

   angry, ironic, detached, sympathetic, amused, saddened—the entire range of human emotions.

4. Peter Elbow describes a paradox that exists in all creative work: "Writing calls on two skills that are so different they usually conflict with each other: creating and criticizing."

   Describe the role of the creative child or artist during the rehearsal phase:

   To generate as many interesting, wacky, off-the-wall, playful & potentially useful ideas or concepts as possible.

   Describe the role of the adult judge or critic during the rehearsal phase:

   To evaluate the appropriateness, usefulness and potential synergy between various ideas.

   How can the writer keep from having the adult critic stifle the imagination of the creative child?

   Do not be overly judgmental when working to initiate creative concepts.

5. Describe the difference between a media treatment and a media script:

A treatment is a narrative description of what the viewer will see & hear in summary form. A script is a complete, detailed set of instructions on how to produce the program.

General Activity 5.2: Media Program Formats (on page 38)

To the Instructor: There are several ways to involve an entire class in this activity. You might assign various class members a few formats and have them brainstorm Pros and Cons for each. You could have students prepare answers in advance as a homework assignment. Or, have them work with a neighbor.

Then, conduct a class discussion.

Ask for Pros—beginning with the Talking Head format.

Write typical responses on a flip chart. Go through the pros and cons of each format in turn. (Make sure students understand the difference between interview formats using on and off-camera interviewers. See pages 78 and 79 in *The Scriptwriter's Handbook.*)

Try to list several points for each format, similar to those on the following pages. A few issues relate to all formats and should be addressed:

*   Degree to which the format depends on the talents of various on and off-camera participants

*   Cost

*   Production logistics and time to complete

*   Credibility

*   Degree to which the format allows for direct, personal communication with the audience

To Instructor and Individual Student: It's important to realize that much of the variety inherent in media writing comes from the manipulation of only a few generic formats.

Each format possesses strengths and weaknesses—making it more or less suited to specific visual and verbal content. (Sometimes, a format's greatest strength can also be its greatest weakness when poorly executed.) It's also useful to consider the demands each format makes on the writer.

Your selection of formats should be a conscious decision based on a variety of factors ranging from content, to production resources, lead time, dynamics of the viewing situation, the audience and objectives.

A/V Media Program Formats

Format 1: Talking Head

Definition: Speakers who address the camera and deliver content without any visualization.

Pros	Cons
Highly personal use of medium	Does not capitalize on visual aspects of media
Hearing directly from authority or expert—high credibility	Potential to be "dull," "boring," uninteresting
Can be produced quickly	Highly talent dependent; most non-professionals lack skills to do well
	Inexpensive

Format 2: Talking Head with Props

Definition: An on-camera speaker addressing the camera who uses props or other visuals to help communicate the message.

Pros	Cons
Begins to use visual capabilities	Requires more production & planning time
Ideal for certain kinds of "how to" demonstrations	Requires integration of sets, props, staging and camera work
The "set" or stage becomes a participant in the program	Usually requires more post-production editing than talking head program
Still hearing from authority or expert; credibility high	More costly
Still highly personal	Even more talent dependent

Format 3: Visuals & Voice

Definition: An off-camera voice with simultaneous display of related visual content or images. (This is the typical sound-slide show format. Can also be a multi-image or computer-generated presentation.) The combined effect of pictures and sound should work synergistically.

Pros	Cons
Maximizes ability to condense time and space	Less personal: "disembodied voice"
High degree of visualization requires less verbalization	Requires many visuals to sustain pacing
Can integrate variety of visual sources: film, slides, graphics, animation, live video	Visuals should be stylistically compatible; designed for medium and look of program
Usually results in better pacing	Requires detailed script integrating visuals and sound track; thorough pre-production planning
	Usually most effective when professional talent reads narration

Format 4A: Interview (On-camera)

Definition: The on-camera interview features both the interviewer and the interviewee.

Pros	Pros
Spontaneous & candid	Requires continuity: a beginning, middle & end
Reveals personality	Highly talent dependent—need skilled, knowledgeable interviewer
Highly credible	Less control of content than scripted formats
Relatively simple to produce	Can become visually static
Creates empathy with subject	

Format 4B: Interview (Off-camera)

Definition: The off-camera interview features only the subject and his/her answers. Interviewer questions are edited out.

Pros	Pros
Spontaneous & condid	Usually requires variety of viewpoints and several interview subjects
Highly credible	High shooting ratio
High level of human interest	Time-consuming post-production
Does not require on-camera interviewer	Less control of content than with scripted formats
	Longer lead times

Format 5: Dramatization

Definition: Content is scripted as dialogue for actors to deliver by assuming the identity of a character. Ideally, should involve conflict between characters.

Pros	Cons
Excellent for portraying dynamics of human interaction	Highly talent dependent in all production areas—including writing
Strong depiction of character and human nature	Small margin for error; can easily appear "corny" or lacking credibility
Potential for high entertainment value	
Highly involving; many stylistic story-telling possibilities	Costly
	Longer production lead times

Format 6: "Apples & Oranges"

Definition: A free-flowing mixture of two or more of the above formats to meet the communication or training needs of the subject matter and add contrast.

Pros	Cons
Can use specific formats as appropriate; content dictates form	Need to coordinate visual look and narrative styles
Maximizes capabilities of medium	Requires effective transitions moving from format to format
Creates variety; visual and narrative change of pace	May become random or choppy in style
	Complicates production logistics

For more on these program formats, see pages 76 through 80 of *The Scriptwriter's Handbook*.

General Activity 5.3: Advertised or Unadvertised Program Structure (on page 43)

To the instructor: Prior to doing this activity, it is helpful to show the class an example of a program using an advertised structure and one that is unadvertised.

Then, have the class complete the activity, preferably with a neighbor. Give them about 15 minutes. (If you have a large class, you may want to have certain groups complete different sections of the activity.)

Then, conduct a class discussion.

Ask for answers to the two questions first.

Write typical answers on a flip chart. Develop a list similar to that on the following pages.

Then, *ask* for advantages and disadvantages of the advertised and unadvertised structures. After these points are clarified, move on to the next activity for a discussion of questions relating to the overall structure of a program's opening, main body and closing.

To Instructor & Individual Student: Certain programs favor using a highly structured, advertised, linear writing style. Other programs are more effective when the structure is not so apparent to the audience and appears more spontaneous.

Training programs often benefit from advertising the structure so the learner knows what's expected and does not become disoriented as content unfolds.

Programs designed to motivate, persuade or project an image are often more effective when the structure is unadvertised.

Longer programs usually need more advertising of structure than short programs.

As with every other aspect of writing the script, determining which structure is best for a given project should be a conscious decision the writer makes for justifiable reasons.

WHAT TO DO: Brainstorm tools the scriptwriter can use to advertise the program structure to the audience. Think of it as ways of letting the audience know what is coming next and reminding them of where they are throughout the time span of the viewing or listening experience.

Simply tell the audience what the structure will be early in the program

Use graphic devices or titles to indicate movement from one topic to the next

Stop occasionally to review what content has been presented and what is yet to come

Use of recurring visual or verbal analogy or metaphor

Brainstorm techniques you can use to conceal the structure:

Mix formats, allowing transitions between them to flow quickly and happen unannounced

Develop a storyline that involves suspense; ways of keeping the audience wanting to know what will happen next

Move fluidly in time and space so the audience must work a bit to keep up with you

WHAT TO DO: Think about the advantages and disadvantages of advertising the structure to your audience and list below. Then, do the same for the unadvertised structure:

Programs using an **advertised** structure...

Advantages	Disadvantages
Audience knows what to expect	Can become predictable
Audience is oriented throughout the program	"Advertising" structure may take time from real substance
Provides framework for organizing content	Tends to be linear
Appears well-organized to viewers	Lacks surprise and suspense

Programs using an **unadvertised** structure...

Advantages	Disadvantages
Unpredictable; audience does not know what to expect	May become confusing or disorienting
Creates suspense	More demanding on writer
Structure does not need to follow pre-determined linear pattern	More demanding of viewers
Allows for more flexibility	Higher level of risk
Less formal; more spontaneous	

General Activity 5.4: Program Structure—Major Segments (on page 45)

To the instructor: This activity helps focus attention on the major functions of a media presentation's open, main body, and closing, regardless of whether the structure employed is advertised or unadvertised.

Have the class complete the activity, preferably with a neighbor. Give them about 10 minutes. Then, conduct a class discussion.

Ask certain people for their answers to the first question. Ask different participants for their answers to the second and the third question.

Write typical answers on a flip chart. Develop a list similar to those that follow:

To Instructor & Individual Student: While this exercise pertains directly to a linear program, the scriptwriter also confronts these same structural elements when developing a non-linear, interactive presentation. The non-linear, interactive presentation, however, gives the viewer more control of the experience by offering optional paths through the content. This creates additional scriptwriting challenges.

It's also important to recognize that an unadvertised, non-linear structure still must have a rational unfolding of information. While the writer may not want the audience to predict what comes next—there must be an embedded logic as to how the material flows from topic to topic—a beginning, middle and end, each serving its own function.

WHAT TO DO: Brainstorm the functions of each of these major program elements. What should you try to accomplish in your opening, body and closing scenes?

Opening Scenes:

Must introduce subject

Must gain attention

Give audience reason to watch, listen or continue with the media program experience

Should not be too lengthy

Scenes comprising the Body:

Present content in logical (though not necessarily advertised) sequence

Take full advantage of the capabilities of the medium

Avoid or overcome the weaknesses of the chosen medium

Have a sense of pacing & energy—as though moving along

Should keep audience interest; keep giving them a reason to stay with the program

Should have one or more "big" scenes—which focus on the program's most significant content or message

Should have a sense of style that is consistent; or, mixes different styles to achieve purposeful effect

Closing Scenes:

Should never be an afterthought

Should have more imagination and impact than simply a key point summary

Sustain the energy

Provide a sense of completion or closure

Should not be too lengthy

General Activity 5.5: Searching for an Appropriate Way to Tell Your Story (on page 48)

To the Instructor: Divide the class in half. Working in buzz groups or with a neighbor, have one side of class work on column one—kinds of stories; the second on column two—ways to tell a story.
   Then, conduct a class discussion.
   Ask for answers, starting with the first column.
   Write typical answers on a flip chart. Develop lists similar to those on the following page.
   Then, *ask* why organizational media scriptwriters should be so concerned about storytelling.

   To Instructor & Individual Student: Storytelling is the way we can take technical information or dry factual material and infuse it with a warm, human touch. Stories can be told by a narrator, or by on-camera participants—from employees to subject matter experts to the Chairman of the Board. A short, simple anecdote or recollection can be extremely powerful at the right moment in a program. Stories are ways to instruct by example.
   The television medium, in particular, accommodates a wide variety of story-telling techniques—from animation to dance and mime to computer graphics. Given the power of stories to spark the imagination and allow your audience to relate and empathize, always think about how you can make your script more interesting and lively through storytelling technique.
   And remember—there's always more than one well to tell a story—especially when using media. One writer may see an assignment as a documentary "true-life" story, while another will find fantasy and the opportunity for animation in the same content. That's what makes writing an art—not a science.

WHAT TO DO: There are different kinds of stories as well as different ways to tell a story. Develop a list of each in the appropriate column.

Kinds of Stories:	Ways to tell a story:
Anecdotes	Tell It
Fairy Tales	Write it down
Ghost story	Act it out
True-life story	Dance
Love story	Tell through song
Fable	Use mime and motion
Allegory	Photographs
Tragedy	Animation
Biography	
Memoir	

General Activity 5.6: Style—Expressing Point-of-View (on page 50)

To the Instructor: Have the class complete the activity, working alone or with a neighbor. Give them about 5 to 7 minutes.

Then, conduct a class discussion.

Ask for answers in each column.

Write typical answers on a flip chart. Develop lists similar to those on the following page.

To the Instructor & Individual Student: When writing prose, style is mostly determined by voice. For the media writer, style includes voice, but that is only one factor among many. As screenwriter Paul Schrader explains:

> "I am not a writer. I am a screenwriter, which is half a filmmaker. I can't *be* a writer because words are not my code—words and sentences and punctuation. My code is far more elaborate. It has to deal with images, montage, cinematography, editing, sound, music." [Brady, *The Craft of the Screenwriter*, p. 262]

The complete media writer will suggest not only when to use music, but what *style* and *tempo* is most appropriate. If graphics are part of the script, describe the graphic style and execution. When mood is important, describe the type of mood sought and how elements like music, pacing and editing (use of dissolves rather than cuts, for instance) will contribute to the overall effect.

Granted, the director's job is execution. It is the director's prerogative to interpret, embellish or even alter the scriptwriter's suggestions during production. But the more specific the scriptwriter is in establishing a vivid narrative voice and visual style, the more likely the script functions as a cohesive, well-crafted set of instructions on "how to produce this program."

WHAT TO DO: In the space provided, list as many elements effecting the style of a media presentation as you can.

Visual Elements:	Audio & Verbal Elements:
• Motion	• Music
• Sets & Locations	• Narration (voice & style)
• Graphics & type	• Dialogue
• Costume & dress	• Sound effects
• Color, light & intensity	• Silence
• Variation in on or off-camera speakers	• Male or female voice
• Variety of formats	• Delivery of narration
• Special Effects	
• Transitions	
• Changes in camera angle or camera movement	

General Activity 5.7: The Media Treatment (on page 55)

To the Instructor: Conduct a class discussion in which you pose the following questions:

Ask: How will a treatment be of help to clients, content experts and other non-media people involved in script development?

Of what value is the treatment to the director? To the producer?

Of what value is the treatment to the writer?

Through class discussion—generate points similar to those below.

To Instructor & Student: Treatments are invaluable at this stage of the scriptwriting process. They express the writer's emerging vision of what the final viewing experience will be like. They define the overall creative direction for the program—allowing everyone to react positively or negatively to various stylistic elements before investing in writing the complete script.

WHAT TO DO: The treatment is the one writing product you produce at the end of the Rehearsal stage to share with producer, client, content expert and director.

Brainstorm the functions a media treatment serves, its value at this stage in the script development process and list in the space provided.

• Helps overcome script "illiteracy" on the part of client, content experts and other non-media people involved in script development.

• Director can use treatment to identify issues relating to production requirements, logistics, schedules, talent, sets and graphics, editing and other production functions.

• Producer uses treatment and director's estimates of production requirements to develop a preliminary budget.

• Scriptwriter uses treatment as guide during drafting phase to produce first draft script.

CHAPTER 6: DRAFTING THE SHOOTING SCRIPT
Review Activity (on page 61)

To Instructor & Individual Student: This review activity covers material presented in Chapter 6 of *The Scriptwriter's Handbook* text, which deals with generating a first draft of the media script. Feel free to refer to the text when necessary.

Review Activity:

WHAT TO DO: Answer the following questions. Refer to the appropriate chapter in *The Scriptwriter's Handbook* if necessary.

1. Identify at least three ways in which a shooting script goes beyond the media treatment:

    It contains all narration & dialogue

    It describes all visuals & graphics

    It links visual & narrative cues in time

    It provides specific transitions between all scenes

    Uses appropriate media production terminology

2. To describe the viewing experience, or chronological sequence of events, and the relationship between sight and sound cues, the writer uses a special vocabulary known as:

    media production terminology

3. Two standard shooting script formats are:

    dual column or split page format

    motion picture format

4. Aesthetician Susanne Langer describes two types of symbol systems:

    Language communicates through "a linear, discrete successive order" governed by laws of syntax. Langer calls this a:

    "discursive" symbol

    Visual symbol systems, such as painting or sculpture, communicate their meaning simultaneously. Langer calls this a:

    "presentational" symbol

    Which symbol system does the media writer employ?

    "Both"

5. When you want absolute certainty the client's perception of visual images matches your intent, the best technique is to:

    create a storyboard

General Activity 6.1: Artist vs. Judge (on page 62)

To the Instructor: By now, you should have a feel for the personality traits of your class. This activity can take on additional meaning by drawing on those insights. You might, for instance, have those people you feel are more "left brain" oriented, identify the characteristics of the judgmental personality; those who are more "right brain," the characteristics of the artistic personality.

Or, switch them—so those who are most artistically inclined must identify characteristics of the judgmental personality and vice versa.

Or you might want to pair them so you have one of each working together, etc.

Ask for answers, starting with the first column.

Write typical answers on a flip chart. Develop lists similar to those below.

Then, *ask* which personality is most important to the drafting process?

To Instructor & Individual Student: Generating a *first* draft script involves going back and forth between "passion hot and critic cold". When you are first generating a section of script—allow the artist to write freely and uncritically. Once you have something down on paper, then start going back over it more critically.

Shift gears spontaneously as the spirit moves you. Remember the danger here—when a teeter-totter is perfectly balanced, stasis sets in. Writer's block is a similar sort of immobility.

WHAT TO DO: Respond to the dual notions of the "artist" vs. the "critic or judge." What qualities do you associate with the artistic personality? What about the judgmental personality? Jot down as many associations as come to mind—your "gut reactions" to the words. Go for as many associations as you can generate.

Characteristics of the artistic personality:	Characteristics of the critic or judgmental personality:
• Creative	• Strives for perfection
• Flexible	• Rigid; unbending
• Emotional	• Detail-oriented
• Iconoclastic	• Persistent
• Spontaneous	• Likes to follow rules
• Warm & humorous	• Serious and judgmental
• Comfortable with ambiguity	• Cold, aloof
• Open to experiment and new ideas	
• Not bound by tradition; comfortable breaking rules	

1. Which personality are you most comfortable with?

2. Which personality do you think is most important to the drafting process?

    The writing process requires going back and forth between both the creative and critical personality. At some point, each must have its say.

General Activity 6.2: Two Common Shooting Script Formats (on page 66)

To the Instructor: Review the Two-Column Video and Motion Picture Script formats, using the sample scripts on pages 64 and 65. Then give the class an opportunity to answer the questions about each script.

Rather than making it a written exercise, you may simply pose each question.

Ask for answers to each and discuss as appropriate.

To Instructor & Individual Student: If you are new to scriptwriting, don't let page formats and production terminology intimidate you. And especially, don't let them slow you down when you are in a "passion hot" moment. It's a lot like spelling and grammar. You can always go back and straighten out the formats or correct your use of production terminology.

Work with both formats. Experiment with them. Find which you prefer. Ideally, the experienced scriptwriter should be capable of using either format—or variations on the format based on the preferences of clients, producers and directors. Only working with these formats will make you comfortable with them. So—dive in.

WHAT TO DO: After reading the two sample scripts, answer the following questions:

1. Which script format do you think is easier for a client, content expert or others not used to reading scripts to visualize how the program will flow as a viewing experience?

    _____ Two-Column Video   _X_ Motion Picture Format

    (With the two-column format, novice script readers often focus on only the narration and dialogue. As such, they mistakenly think this is where all the content is. In a well-written script, much of the content should be in the visuals. The motion picture format forces people to read the visual descriptions; or, at least, makes it more difficult to ignore them.)

2. Beginning scriptwriter's often make the mistake of writing narration or dialogue first—then the pictures. Which script format do you think encourages this approach?

    _X_ Two-Column Video   _____ Motion Picture Format

    (The two-column format may encourage the writer to do the narration—then go back and fill in the visuals. A dangerous habit to get into. Script visuals and narration as you progress. Always write with pictures in mind.)

3. Which script format do you think most precisely shows the exact relationship between audio and visual cues?

    _X_ Two-Column Video   _____ Motion Picture Format

    (This is the major strength of the two-column format. Cues coordinating picture and sound can be indicated quite precisely on the page.)

4. From a word-processing standpoint, which format do you think is most user-friendly?

    _____ Two-Column Video   _X_ Motion Picture Format

    (The motion picture format is easier to set up and work with. Once you develop a template for the two-column format, however, and become familiar with using it, neither format is overly burdensome to work with.)

General Activity 6.3: The 60-Second Benchmark (on page 66)

To the Instructor: Have the class complete the activity—working alone or with a neighbor. Give them about 5 to 7 minutes.

Conduct a class discussion.

Ask for answers in each column.

Write typical responses on a flip chart. You should build a list similar to that below.

To Instructor & Individual Student: Repetition and sameness in pacing lead to predictability. This is often what causes audiences to say a media program is "boring."

In general, there are more opportunities for the writer to vary pacing visually than through the sound track. Music of different tempos and styles can often be used to signal changes in pace.

Ultimately, pacing is controlled by the director's execution of the script. Scriptwriters, however, need to be aware of pacing as the draft script emerges.

At some point, the writer needs to look at the overall pacing of the program in relation to each scene or content point. Pacing within each scene can also be examined shot by shot.

If you find each page, or sixty seconds, of your script has four basic shots or graphics—ask what you can do to achieve greater variety to generate audience interest through more sophisticated use of pacing.

WHAT TO DO: If pacing is the rate at which visual and auditory events change—list those sight and sound elements available to the scriptwriter for changing the pace. What visual and auditory tools do you have to effect change. Which elements of change are within your control as writer?

VISUAL ELEMENTS:	AUDITORY ELEMENTS:
Shots	Changes in music
Relationship of camera to subject	Change in speaker
Transitions & special visual effects	Changes in narrative style
Changes in scenes, sets, locations	Changes in dynamics (soft to loud, etc.)
Movement within the frame (also camera movement)	Changes in tempo (fast to slow speech pattern; slow to up-tempo music)
Color vs. b&w	Sound effects
Changes in graphics or artwork	Counterpoint (music & narration at same time; music & sound effects, etc.)
Animation	
Posterization or other graphic special effect	

Now, answer these questions, keeping the sixty-second rule-of-thumb in mind:

1. Writing using the dual column format, you notice you have a full page of narration and a single shot description. What does this tell you about your pacing?

   This seems like a relatively static shot. Unless there is movement within the frame; or a static shot is motivated (perhaps it's an executive message that does not require visualization) you should consider including more shots to visualize the narration. Consider also, if you use more visuals, can you shorten narration?

2. You are on page 8 of a script that is ten minutes long. Where should you be in terms of the overall arc of the program?

About to move from the main body to the closing.

3. What if you still have significant content to communicate?

You are facing a time problem. Are you being realistic about the time required to communicate key content? Or, have you over-written narration? Can you simplify and shorten narrative copy? Have visuals carry more of the message? These are the issues you must address. Perhaps you want to conclude the script in its present style, however, to determine how much of a time problem you face.

4. What is the difference in pacing between a shot in which the screen is static and a shot in which the screen action is continuously changing?

A shot in which the screen action changes provides inherent visual variety. This type of shot can usually remain on screen for a longer time period than a totally static shot.

CHAPTER 7: IMAGINATIVE WRITING FOR EYE & EAR
Review Activity (on page 69)

To Instructor & Individual Student: This review activity covers material presented in chapters 7 and 8 of *The Scriptwriter's Handbook* text, focusing on techniques of writing for the eye and ear. So be sure to read both chapters before answering this review. Feel free to refer to the appropriate chapter text when necessary.

1. Identify three visualization problems beginning media writers sometimes experience:

   Verbal Dominance

   "Kitchen Sink" Syndrome

   Inappropriate Visualization

2. To overcome these problems, identify three "Guidelines for Effective Visualization"

   Make Stylistic Decisions Early

   Determine Function of Visuals

   Identify Big "Building Blocks"

3. Many camera directions media writers use in a script describe the changing relationship between the *camera* and the *subject*.

4. Describe the difference between these common visual transitions used in a variety of media:

   A. Fade Up; or, Fade to Black

   B. Dissolve

In a fade, the picture gradually appears from black (Fade Up) or disappears to black. In a dissolve, two scenes briefly overlap, one fading in, the other fading out. Dissolves usually signal changes in time or location.

C. Dissolve

D. Wipe

A wipe differs from a dissolve in that it has a hard edge as one picture replaces another. A wipe can move across, diagonally, or up and down the screen.

5. According to Murray, what is the element of a story that "carries its emotional force?"

Voice

6. Read over the following descriptions of media program subjects or topics within a media program. Then, decide whether the subject is best suited to a professional narrator or a company spokesperson. Enter "P" for Professional Narrator; "CS" for Company Spokesperson:

    CS   Explanation of why your company has been acquired by another.

    P   Detailed description of company benefit plans.

    CS   Expression of company's commitment to provide competitive benefits.

    P   Explanation of how new Food & Drug Administration (FDA) guidelines effect a pharmaceutical company's Physician Speakers Program.

    CS   Statement of that pharmaceutical company's commitment to abide by FDA Guidelines.

    P   Training program on principles of credit management.

7. Narration is the "workhorse" of corporate and documentary media presentations. What are four general categories of narrative copy identified in Chapter 8 of *The Scriptwriter's Handbook*?

    On-camera

    Off-camera

    Executive or Subject Matter Expert Presentation

    Character Narrations

8. What is the primary function of music in a media production?

    To help communicate the emotional tone, set mood, cue transitions, etc.

9. In the early days of radio, writers challenged their listening audiences to imagine the action of a radio drama in the mind's eye. This prompted radio writers to refer to their medium as *theatre* of the imagination.

WHAT TO DO: The following activity will give you practice using this scriptwriting language...

General Activity 7.2: Writing Camera Directions

BACKGROUND: If you've never written camera directions before, this exercise gives you practice.

WHAT TO DO: The illustration below depicts the view from a writer's woodland retreat. (The antique object on the table is a manual typewriter. No batteries needed!) Read the description of "where the shot begins" and "where the shot ends." Then, write an appropriate camera direction in the space provided. Refer to the list of common camera directions if you find them helpful.

CU on stream. Camera zooms out to reveal desk and portraits on wall.

Where shot begins: the camera includes only the stream outside the window. . .
Where shot ends: a complete view of the desk and portraits on wall.

Write an appropriate description of the shot and movement of camera (or lens) to arrive at the ending shot.

CU on Dickens portrait. Pan left to CU on Emily Dickinson.

Where shot begins: the camera is focused on the portrait of Charles Dickens to the right of the window.
Where shot ends: the camera moves to focus on the portrait of Emily Dickinson to the left of the window.

Write an appropriate description of the shot and movement of camera (or lens) to arrive at the ending shot.

CU on stream. Tilt down to CU on typewriter.

Where shot begins: the camera includes only the stream outside the window. . .
Where shot ends: shot shows only the typewriter.

Write an appropriate description of the shot and movement of the camera (or lens) to arrive at the ending shot.

LS on desk and portraits. Camera zooms in and pans left to CU on Emily Dickinson portrait.

Where shot begins: camera shows entire scene. . .
Where shot ends: a shot showing only portrait of Emily Dickinson left of the window.

Write an appropriate description of the shot and movement of the camera (or lens) to arrive at the ending shot.

General Activity 7.3: Writing for the Ear (on page 76)

To the Instructor: Answering these questions will get students thinking about the special needs of writing narration or dialogue.

To Instructor & Individual Student: Difficulties with writing narration can almost always be traced to lack of conversational style. Therefore, reading copy aloud is the best way to find areas that need to be reworked in a more conversational style. There are several ways of doing this. Experiment until you find what works best for you.

WHAT TO DO: Answer the following questions.

1. Brainstorm ways in which writing narration—words for other people to read as others listen—differs from writing words meant to be read by a reader on paper.

   Sentences must be shorter—so they can be read aloud without running out of breath

   Use of contractions to help create a conversational style

   Generally more personal; on-camera narrator speaks directly to viewer and can address as "you"

   Conversational style should take precedence over grammatical correctness

   Certain combinations of words or syllables may present difficulty when spoken out loud

   As a general rule, sentence structure cannot be as complex

2. Given all these factors, what do you think is the "acid test" for your own narrative copy?

   Read it aloud

3. What are several ways of doing this?

   Read it aloud to yourself

   Have someone else read it aloud for you

   Read it aloud into a tape recorder; then play it back to yourself

General Activity 7.4: The Power of Voice (on page 77)

To the Instructor: You may want to assign this activity on developing a range of voices for homework. Give the class an example beforehand so they get the sense of how far they can take this exercise.
   Make sure they select voices they are comfortable with and that those voices are distinctive.
   Have students read their work aloud in class. Probe to find out how they approached the activity, what they experienced doing it, and how they think this technique can help them develop as writers.

To Instructor & Individual Student: This writing exercise will strengthen your ability to write in many voices. It's especially useful when working on characterization and dialogue.
   Be bold in doing this activity. Let yourself go. Have fun with it. Choose voices you know well and can mentally lock into. Your ability to find the appropriate voice for each script you write is an important aspect of becoming a versatile, professional writer; one who brings variety and fresh perspectives to

each project. It's also vital for writing dialogue and developing distinctive on-screen characters when you choose the dramatization format.

Ideally, as you rewrite the "corporate helvetica text," you should find that words, syntax and speech rhythms change as you adopt different voices.

WHAT TO DO: Do two rewrites of the following "voiceless" prose (taken from an executive speech) by selecting from the menu of voices listed below. Check two voices that are quite diverse—as well as voices you know well.

VOICE SELECTION MENU

✔ **Dolly Parton**   ____ **Bill Cosby**

____ **Norm or Cliff (from Cheers)**   ____ **A Pirate King**

____ **Bart, Homer or Marge Simpson**   ____ **A "Street Smart" Homeless Person**

____ **Murphy Brown**   ____ **A "Jock" or Hayden Fox (from Coach)**

____ **Miss Piggy or Kermit the Frog**   ____ **A "Valley Girl" or Phoebe (from Friends)**

✔ **Other (Identify: Woody Allen)**

Identify the two different voices you will assume in rewriting the Executive Speech Text. In doing this activity, **exaggerate** your use of voice. The more distinctive you make it—the better.

Rewrite #1: Voice Selection: Dolly Parton

Text: "Why with satellites wizzin' around up in the heavens and jumbo jets takin' off and landin' every minute— this old world's shrinkin' up more everyday. Why, seems like I can record a song in Nashville one day—then hear it on the radio in Hollywood workin' on a movie set the next.

"Songs are written on computer screens and television's everywhere I roam around the world. Makes ya kinda realize how we're all part of the same family tree on this little ole planet called earth..."

Rewrite #2: Voice Selection: Woody Allen

Text: "As a kid growing up in Brooklyn, my parents weren't exactly world travelers. Like—going to Queens was a big outing. And a trip into Manhattan—well, that was enough excitement for six months.

"One year, though, we did take a real family vacation. Drove all the way to Jersey City to stay three days with the Beatleman's. I was disoriented the whole time. I mean the city skyline was on the wrong side of the river.

"These days, friends in the film business think nothing of flying back and forth from East Coast to left coast three or four times a week. Talk about anxiety! I'd worry my mouth would be in L.A. while my dentist worked on my teeth in New York. Like, what state would you file your insurance claim in?"

CHAPTER 8: REVISING & EDITING THE SCRIPT
Review Activity 8 (on page 81)

To Instructor & Individual Student: This last review activity covers material presented in chapter 9 of *The Scriptwriter's Handbook* text, focusing on revision strategies. Feel free to refer to the text when necessary.

1. "Revision" means: *to see again.*

2. Only the writer relates to the shooting script as both *writer* and *reader.*

3. In evaluating each individual script reader's feedback, media writers need to consider three related factors:

   When does it occur in the writing process?

   Who does the feedback come from?

   What is the substance of the feedback?

4. When the client or Subject Matter Expert identifies a relevant, valid shortcoming in the first draft script, you should consider this a:

   Genuine objection

5. What is the difference between a "Genuine" and a "Hopeless" objection?

   There are many different ways of responding to and resolving the genuine objection. The hopeless objection implies there is no point in trying to defend your position. The client's mind is made up.

6. When you first hear a genuine objection, you may totally agree or disagree. Name two other probable initial responses:

   You may be uncertain.

   You may be confused.

7. Why should you try to anticipate objections to a work in progress?

   To analyze its validity and prepare a well-considered response in advance.

General Activity 8.1: "Seeing Again" (on page 82)

To the Instructor: One way to do this activity is to divide the class in half. Give one half the assignment of brainstorming associations with the word "feedback," the other half associating with "rejection." You may further divide the class into buzz groups or have them work with a neighbor.

Give them about four to five minutes.

Conduct a class discussion, bringing up associations similar to those noted on the answer sheet. Jot down answers on flip chart.

Then, develop a response to the second question as a group, based on the associations you arrived at.

To Instructor & Individual Student: Aspiring writers are often familiar with the form letter rejection slip. This standardized "thanks but no thanks" can be crushing, especially to beginning writers. Having invested considerable time, energy and personal commitment in a work of writing, it is deflating to be rejected by an editor, publisher, agent, producer or the like.

Therefore, it's important to develop a more positive attitude toward the feedback one receives from clients, producers, directors and subject matter experts on a media script. These are collaborative projects. Such feedback is part of the process. Generally, you'll find it helpful, constructive and useful in making the next draft an improvement.

Occasionally, you may feel strongly that the feedback you're receiving is dead wrong or misguided. Later in this chapter, we'll look at ways to categorize objections and develop responses. It's important to realize, however, that sometimes you face a "no-win" situation. Recognize the situation as such. Part of the creative process is knowing when and how to "let go." There will be other opportunities in the future. Do the best you can in a bad situation. Preserve professionalism.

WHAT TO DO: Distinguish between "feedback" and "rejection" by entering your associations to the two words in the space provided. What's the difference between the two?

FEEDBACK:	REJECTION:
Expresses valuable viewpoint	Expresses disappointment; implies failure
Offers a fresh perspective	Damages ego
An expression of interest	Assertion of power & dominance
Implies progress toward a goal	Shows lack of appreciation of work
Helpful & constructive	Harmful & destructive
A necessary step in an evolving process	Implies an end to the process
Can be motivating	Is often demotivating

Difference between the two:

Feedback is positive & constructive. Rejection has many negative connotations. The writer's attitude toward criticism, however, may be the difference in whether criticism is perceived as "feedback" or "rejection." Try to keep an open mind so reactions of collaborators are viewed as constructive input—a necessary step in the process.

General Activity 8.2: Presenting the First Draft Script (on page 85)

To the Instructor: First, use the figure on script reader perspectives as a quick way of reviewing the varying viewpoints each reader brings to the evaluation of a first draft script.

Then, have the class consider pros and cons of two ways of presenting the draft script. You might ask half the class to develop a response to question one while the other half responds to question two.

Give them about four to five minutes.

Conduct a class discussion, bringing up issues noted on the answer sheet.

To Instructor & Individual Student: The question of how best to present clients with the first draft shooting script harkens back to an earlier activity where script readers were identified. Often, clients and subject matter experts have difficulty visualizing a viewing experience from the printed page.

One way to minimize confusion—have the writer present the first draft in a meeting which includes client, subject matter experts, producer and director.

Generally, the script is read aloud—although certain special effects or camera directions may be explained more fully. This meeting is also a good time to present a sketch of a set, special graphic treatments or storyboards of visually complex sections.

Most writers prefer to present first draft scripts in person. Sometimes, however, time and travel schedules preclude a script presentation meeting. Or, clients and subject matter experts with experience and sophistication reading scripts will want an opportunity to read in advance—allowing everyone to prepare comments and get to an immediate discussion of feedback.

Either way, once presented, the initial feedback from your script readers moves you into the revision stage of the writing process.

WHAT TO DO: Describe the perspective and focus of each script reader in the space provided in each box.

Figure 14 Script Reader Perspectives	
Client: Results	**Producer:** Results, Cost, Logistics
Content Expert: Technical Accuracy	**Director:** How do I turn this into a viewing experience?

WHAT TO DO: Consider the pros and cons of two common ways to present first draft shooting scripts by answering the following questions:

1. Sometimes, the draft shooting script is circulated among the principal script readers prior to a joint meeting so they all have time to respond individually and make notes on questions and concerns.

   List advantages of this approach:

   All script readers can prepare their comments for the meeting

   Script reader responses will not be influenced by reactions of others

   Saves time

   List disadvantages of this approach:

   Some readers may have difficulty integrating sight and sound elements

   Technical production jargon may be confusing

   First impressions may color overall objectivity

2. A second method is to call all principal script readers to a meeting where the writer presents the script by reading it aloud, getting a general response, then giving everyone an opportunity for individual, detailed review following the meeting.

List advantages of this approach:

Special effects, visuals and matters of interpretation can be clarified in person

All readers respond to an identical presentation of the script

List disadvantages of this approach:

Readers may be prone to give "knee jerk" responses

One dominant individual may influence reactions of others

Detailed feedback will have to wait for more thorough review; could require a second meeting

General Activity 8.3: Feedback Situations for Analysis (on page 87)

To the Instructor: You may want to have groups of participants respond to different situations. Give them about 5 to 8 minutes to brainstorm responses among themselves. Then, conduct a class discussion, bringing out issues noted on the answer sheet.

To Instructor & Individual Student: All these situations involve analyzing who is presenting the feedback in conjunction with the timing of the feedback in the script development process as well as the content of the comments. Some of these situations should be avoided by developing documents such as content outline, audience profile, objectives and treatment.

No matter what the situation, it's always important to hear objections out in their entirety. Sometimes, this calls for patience and tact. Those are qualities that make a writer professional—especially in this collaborative arena.

WHAT TO DO: To help apply these principles, answer the following case study questions.

1. The content expert offers feedback on the style of the script. What are some key considerations in analyzing his or her feedback?

   Content experts may or may not have a realistic sense of the target audience and the communication environment. Ultimately, matters of style should be approved by the client and producer—not the subject matter expert.

2. The director offers feedback indicating concern over the feasibility of producing the script within budget or on schedule. What are key considerations in analyzing his or her feedback?

   First, did the director raise these concerns when the treatment was presented? If so, they should have been addressed at that time. Try to determine if there are ways to simplify production without changing the overall concept. How serious is the budgetary overrun or scheduling problem? Is there room for negotiating these points with client and producer?

3. The client feels that the finished program, as written, will simply not fulfill his or her expectations. What are key considerations in analyzing his or her feedback?

Did the client completely "buy into" the creative concept as expressed in the treatment? If so, are there differences between the treatment and the execution of the script? Also, is there disagreement or confusion over the objectives of the program? Perhaps the discussion should begin by having the client restate his/her expectations for the program.

4. The content expert feels that you have not fully understood one segment of the content. He or she has rewritten that segment. What are key considerations in analyzing this feedback and how should you respond?

The content expert is showing genuine interest in the project's success. However, the content expert's rewrite may pose certain stylistic problems or require better visualization, etc. Make sure you understand the content issue at stake. Thank the content expert for his/her time and input; then re-work that input so it flows seamlessly into the script.

5. Because of a company reorganization, you now have a new client who has not participated in any of the previous developmental work. The client is not at all satisfied with the creative approach. What are key considerations in analyzing this feedback?

Unfortunately, the new client has the right to stop the project in mid-stream and reconsider the overall approach. That will almost always mean a delay in the production schedule. If a freelance writer or producer has been engaged, they are entitled to some additional fee since they are being asked to do additional work through no fault of their own.

General Activity 8.4: Identifying Objections (on page 88)

To the Instructor: You may want to have students do this short activity individually.
Give them about 5 minutes.
Then, conduct a class discussion, bringing out issues noted on the answer sheet.

To Instructor & Individual Student: On the surface, this activity seems to be about identifying different types of objections. The underlying point, however, is that only the "genuine objection" requires serious analysis and discussion.
"Minor objections" can easily be fixed in a second draft.
"Hopeless objections" mean the current approach is probably going to be altered so radically, it will mean returning to the rehearsal step to re-think the project.

WHAT TO DO: Listed below are several responses you might have to an objection raised in a script review. Write out the type of objection you think this response relates most closely to in the space provided:

1. You listen carefully to the feedback, but decide you should probe with follow-up questions to clarify. What type of objection are you most likely dealing with?

Genuine Objection

2. You decide you should counter the objection or concern, offering your perspective on why the revision is not appropriate. What type of objection are you most likely dealing with?

Genuine Objection

3. You buy time for more consideration of the objection or concern. What type of objection are you most likely dealing with?

Genuine Objection

4. What does this tell you about what types of objections are worth responding to?

Only the genuine objection merits careful analysis, clarification, discussion and, perhaps, negotiation.

General Activity 8.5: Editing the Shooting Script (on page 91)

To the Instructor: You may simply want to ask these questions of your class, discussing them as various people offer answers.

To Instructor & Individual Student: In a sense, writing always involves identifying and solving problems. In the editing phase, the questions you need to ask become far more detailed than those you posed earlier in the writing process.

By answering these questions, you begin to polish the script, so minor problems with style, length, and accuracy are addressed and corrected. As a general rule, this is when you should seek to tighten the script, since most writers tend to over-write. Remember: "less is more."

Don't lose sight of the fact that your goal is to create the most useful set of instructions to the production team on how to produce this media presentation. You are not editing a document that will be printed, published and read by your target audience.

WHAT TO DO: What are the types of decisions and choices you should be making when you reach the third and fourth draft? Brainstorm the kinds of choices you think you should be focusing on at this stage of the writing process. List in the space provided:

1. What type of choices should you be focusing on in the third and fourth draft?

Is the "voice" and visual style consistent?

Is narration & dialogue as tight and conversational as possible?

Are there any momentary lapses in clarity?

2. What is your goal at this stage of the writing process?

To prepare the script for production by improving on the first and second drafts.

3. How does editing a media script differ from the editorial process used in editing print copy? How is it similar? Enter your ideas in the space provided:

How is editing a media script similar to editing print copy	In what ways does editing a media script differ from editing print copy
Requires objectivity	Does not necessarily need to be grammatically perfect (shot directions or graphic descriptions, for instance)
Requires attention to detail	Does not need to be "speced" for typesetting
Requires the analytical skills of the "judge"	Punctuation of narration or dialogue will convey sense of spoken word
	The script in printed form will ultimately become obsolete; a text lives on in its printed form

Thoughts for Moving Forward

"All writing begins in confusion." On the one hand, that confusion and the need to bring order is the writer's "raison d'etre." Yet, this initial confusion can also overwhelm the writer. We feel the project is beyond our capabilities. Or we will never finish by the deadline. Or that we have nothing new to give to this subject and audience.

Uncertainty and self-doubt come with the territory. Paradoxically, this is both a joy and frustration. It's what keeps a writer's work fresh.

Engage in the Process

The best way to overcome such self-doubts? Actively engage in the writing process—one step at a time; one decision at a time. Initially, decisions are on a macro level. By the end of the process we are down to choosing between one word or another. Tweaking the text of a graphic title. Making a deletion to improve pacing.

If you are new to scriptwriting, you may assume that in the future you'll be capable of beginning a project without the accompanying angst. Unfortunately, (or fortunately) it simply doesn't work that way. As your craft matures and grows, so, too, does your urge for taking bolder risks; daring something totally new and untried.

Move Forward

In the movie *Annie Hall*, Woody Allen makes this observation: "A relationship is like a shark. It has to keep moving forward or it dies. Annie, I think we've got a dead shark on our hands."

Writer's, like sharks, must keep moving forward. At times, you'll find this constant forward motion a source of frustration and weariness. At other times, it brings a rush of exhilaration; a natural high.

Nonetheless, each new project begins with confusion and the same, haunting question: "Can I write this?"

About the Author

BILL VAN NOSTRAN, author of *The Scriptwriter's Handbook*, is an award-winning writer and Senior Writer at Video Marketing Group, Inc., a firm offering video and multi-media production services. His clients include major companies in diverse industries such as AT&T, Prudential, International Paper, Kraft, Johnson & Johnson Philip Morris, Coopers & Lybrand, Warner-Lambert and many others.

Bill has extensive experience writing major meetings and business theatre evens as well as works for the legitimate stage. His play, *Dream Machines*, won several awards including a New Jersey State Council on the Arts fellowship. Bill conducts workshops on scriptwriting and the creative process and teaches in the MBA program at Fairleigh Dickinson University.